HEALING GOD'S WAY

The Art of Spiritual Warfare, Healing, and Deliverance

Devotional

Da'Naia Jackson

DEDICATION

I dedicate this devotional to Jehovah the Most High God, let His praises continually be in my mouth all the days of my life.

And the Lord the Father, Son and Holy Spirit said to me, to begin with:

Deuteronomy 9:11-29

"At the end of those forty days and forty nights, The Lord gave me two tablets of stone, the Tablets of the Covenant. And the Lord said to me, "Hurry, go down from here at once, for the people whom you brought out of Egypt have acted wickedly; they have been quick to stray from the path that I enjoined upon them; they have made themselves a molten image." The Lord further said to me, "I see that this is a stiff-necked people. Let Me alone and I will destroy them and blot out their name from under the heaven, and I will make you a nation far more numerous than they." I started down the mountain, a mountain ablaze with fire, the two Tablets of the Covenant in my two hands. I saw how you had sinned against the Lord your God: you had made yourselves a molten calf; you had been quick to stray from the path that the Lord had enjoined upon you. Thereupon I gripped the two tablets and flung them away with both my hands, smashing them before your eyes. I threw myself down before the Lord, eating no bread and drinking no water for forty days and forty nights, as before because of the great wrong you committed, doing what displeased the Lord and vexing Him. For I was in dread of the Lord's fierce anger against you, which moved Him to wipe you out. And that time, too, the Lord gave heed to me. Moreover, the Lord was angry enough with Aaron to have destroyed him; so I also interceded for Aaron at that time. As for that

sinful thing you had made, the calf, I took it and put it in the fire; I broke it to bits and ground it thoroughly until it was fine as dust, and I threw it into the brook that comes down from the mountain. Again, you provoked the Lord at Taberah and at Massah, and at Kibroth-hattaavah. And when the Lord sent you on from Kadesh-barnea, saying, "Go up and take possession of the land that I am giving you," you flouted the command of the Lord your God; you did not put your trust in Him and did not obey Him. As long as I have known you, you have been defiant toward the Lord. When I lay prostrate before the Lord these forty days and forty nights, because the Lord was determined to destroy you, I prayed the Lord and said, "Oh Lord God, do not annihilate Your very own people, whom you redeemed in Your majesty and whom you freed from Egypt with a mighty hand. Give thought to your servants, Abraham, Isaac and Jacob, and pay no heed to the stubbornness of this people, it's wickedness and sinfulness. Else the country in which you freed us will say, "it was because the Lord was powerless to bring them into the land that He had promised them, and because He rejected them, that He brought them out to have them die in the wilderness.' Yet they are Your very own people, whom You freed with Your great might and Your outstretched arm."- JPS Tanakh

Acknowledgments

Proverbs 3:6

In all your ways acknowledge Him, and He will make your paths smooth - JPS

I confess with my mouth and believe in my heart that Jesus Christ is Lord and commit this work to the Lord so my plans will be established. I confess that without the Father, Son and Holy Spirit, nothing in this work would be possible; therefore, all praise, honor and glory belong to Him for entrusting me with this devotion.

For of Him and through Him and to Him are all things, to whom be glory forever. Amen- Romans 11:36 NKJV

CONTENTS

These owner of this book is Submerged and Sealed with the Blood of the Lord Jesus Christ.

INTRODUCTION

Ah! I'm so excited to join you on this journey of your personal Healing and Deliverance through the Art of Spiritual warfare. Now, I know a great deal of you reading this are hearing the terms healing, deliverance and spiritual warfare for the first time with hesitation if this is right for you. The other group of people reading have some knowledge about these concepts and are looking for additional guidance and support to receive their complete freedom.

In both cases, you've taken a step in your journey to elevate to the next level of your life with breakthroughs and solutions. In brief, I would like to encourage you as you go through each page of this devotional over the next 40 days and nights with a word from *Hebrews 12:1-2:*

> *Therefore we also, since we are surrounded by so great a cloud of witnesses, let us lay aside every weight, and the sin which so easily ensnares us, and let us run with endurance the race that is set before us, looking unto Jesus, the author and finisher of our faith, who for the joy that was set before Him endured the cross, despising the shame, and has sat down at the right hand of the throne of God.-NKJV*

In this race, know that you, yes you, are not alone, but that you have fellow members of the body of Christ past, present and future who have passed through trials, tribulations and tests of life and still press on toward the goal for the prize of the upward call of God in Christ Jesus.

I come to you as a witness in testimony who has experienced exceptional pain, trauma and bondage - emotionally, physically and spiritually. However, even throughout those experiences, I've learned how to lay aside every weight, from childhood trauma, rape, death of my father, rejection, infidelity, self-hate, shame, guilt, and much more, through a purging process of getting raw, real and naked with God, leaving nothing unsaid to Him about what I have gone through.

One piece of the word that I held on to during this process was *2 Corinthians 4:8-10: We are hard-pressed on every side, yet not crushed; we are perplexed, but not in despair; persecuted, but not forsaken; struck down, but not destroyed - always carrying about in the body the dying of the Lord Jesus, that the life of Jesus also may be manifested in our body.-NKJV*

I was inspired to write this devotional in prayer and supplication to the Lord in faith that the Holy Spirit will bear witness with your spirit so you can receive the healing and deliverance that you've been longing for. I pray also that it serves as a form of revelation, that as a believer in Christ Jesus our Lord, you will have hard, draining, unfair, brutal and devastating life experiences. Furthermore, those life experiences will have you feeling like you'll never survive, you're crushed and destroyed, you'll always be broke, you'll always be single, you'll always struggle, that no one has ever cared about you or helped you, and many more I know that you can identify with.

The truth, however, is two-fold.

> *My God shall supply all your need according to His riches in glory by Christ Jesus. Philippians 4:19-NKJV*

> *Moreover, The Lord is near to those who have a broken heart, and saves such as have a contrite spirit. Psalm 34:18 NKJV*

And in this state is when you are so weak and tired and do not have the strength to try, which is the sweetest place for The Lord to come in because *His grace is sufficient for you, for His strength is made perfect in weakness. 2 Corinthians 12:9 NKJV*

The process in which you will go through in this devotional is designed to expose the state of your broken heart and remorseful spirit to the Lord, giving Him full access to all your cares, worries and anxieties. Day and night for 40 days, you will be provoked to get raw, real and naked with our Lord Jesus Christ through a series of repentance, renunciation, and confessions to strengthen your spirit man, healing and deliverance, prayers, and scripture.

Each day has a prompt to be answered during the day and one to be answered at night. I highly recommend setting aside time to complete the day prompt first thing in the morning before you do anything else, and the night as the last thing you do before going to bed.

You may experience some physical body responses, such as extreme exhaustion, tingling as you recite the prayers out loud, dry mouth, burping, farting, vomiting and tears, which are all normal and signs of deliverance. I recommend having some paper towels, tissues, a small trash can, and easy access to a restroom available in the event that you begin to experience any of these symptoms during your devotion time.

The Holy Spirit is ready to meet you in the climax of your broken heart and contrite spirit. He's ready to save you and forgive you for your rebellion and disobedience against Him. He's ready to heal you, deliver you, guide you, protect you and give you an abundance of life. By committing to this devotional, you are taking the first step in meeting our Lord and Savior in the secret place and allowing Him to be first in your life.

The number 40 is significant as it is a number of testing frequently used in the word of God. The next 40 days and nights is your test with the Lord, and your desire and faith in Him to see you through will be exposed, pushing you to the breakthrough you have been requesting of Him.

Now I release the voice of the blood of Jesus over you and break the yoke and bar from upon you, and I tear off your shackles in Jesus' mighty name. I release the Spirit of the Lord God upon you because the Lord has anointed me to bring the good news to the afflicted. Therefore, I bind up - with the 7 chains of the Holy Spirit - the brokenhearted to proclaim liberty to captives and freedom to prisoners. In Jesus' name. Amen.

I release the blessing of the Lord upon your life and look forward to hearing your testimony.

Get ready, Set, Go!

These Devotions and Prayers are Submerged and Sealed with the Blood of the Lord Jesus Christ.

DAY 1

The Physician

Mark 2:17

"When Jesus heard it, He said to them, "Those who are healthy have no need of a physician, but [only] those who are sick; I did not come to call the righteous, but sinners, to repentance.""- AMP

(Mark 13-17; Matt.9.9-13; Luke 5:27-32)

"Then He went out again by the sea; and all the multitude came to Him, and He taught them. As He passed by, He saw Levi, the son of Alphaeus sitting at the tax office. And He said to him, "Follow Me," so he arose and followed Him"-NKJV

"Now it happened, as He was dining in Levi's house, that many tax collectors and sinners also sat together with Jesus and His disciples; for there were many, and they followed Him. And when the scribes and Pharisees saw Him eating with the tax collectors and sinners, they said to His disciples, "How is it that He eats and drinks with tax collectors and sinners?"-NKJV

First, we see that Jesus went out and an innumerable amount of people came to Him. The "key" is that people sought or in Hebrew "baqash" pronounced (baw-kash) - Strong's Concordance 1245 meaning to seek or looking.

Therefore, a mass of people with intention went looking for him, and they found Him. And He taught them. The desperation these people had in their situations had them seeking Him. And when you seek, you shall find.

And you will seek Me and find Me, when you search for Me with all your heart – Jeremiah 29:13 NKJV

Next, you see that as Jesus passed by, ministering to the people, He saw someone (Levi) sitting in the tax office. Levi sitting in the tax office is representative of a sinner sitting in the midst of his sin, yet, the Lord and our savior Jesus Christ spotted him and spoke, "Follow Me."

This is significant because, in this time, from the Jewish perspective and meaning, tax collectors were considered traders to the Jewish culture for collecting taxes for the Romans who occupied that territory. Working as a tax collector was looked down upon, separating them from the law and the beliefs of the prophets, warranting that person a scarlet letter "S" - identifying them a perpetual sinner. However, Levi sitting in the midst of his sin was called by Jesus to "Follow Me," and immediately there was an action of Levi arising and following Him. For as it is written, *No one can come to Me unless the Father who sent Me draws him; and I will raise him up at the last day. John 6:44 NKJV*

Thus, when our Savior Jesus Christ calls you, it is because The Father in heaven has drawn you to Christ. And sometimes, that draw comes with conviction in the midst of our sin from the Spirit of God to repentance. Recognizing the draw and conviction of the Holy Spirit comes in many ways. For example, ignoring that "gut feeling" that you should or should not do something, along with many more.

Admitting that you are in need of Jesus is the First step!

What are you holding on to that the Lord is calling you away from?

Pre-marital or extra-marital sex, lust, porn, gambling, prostitution, promiscuity, drug addiction, alcoholism, slander, gossip, pedophilia, incest, witchcraft, Satanism, sex addiction, foul mouth, anger issues…etc.

Now is the time to be completely naked with God (in detail) about your situation, even if you're currently in the act of *sin "casting all your care upon Him, for He cares for you"- 1 Peter 5:7 NKJV*

Repeat this prayer out loud: I stand against the spirit of fear, confusion, doubt, anxiety and depression in my life, and I lose myself from every frequency of these spirits and reprogram myself into the power of the blood of Jesus. In Jesus' Mighty name.

Daytime confession:

_____

_____

_____

_____

_____

_____

_____

_____

_____

_____

_____

_____

_____

How do you feel about yourself after your daytime confession?

Shameful, guilty, heavy, sick, disgusted?

Come to Me, all you who labor and are heavy laden, and I will give you rest. Take My yoke upon you and learn from Me, for I am gentle and lowly in heart, and you will find rest for your souls. For My yoke is easy and My burden is light.- Matthew 11:28-30 NKJV

If we confess our sins, He is faithful and just to forgive us our sins and to cleanse us from all unrighteousness. 1 John 1:9 NKJV

Repeat this prayer out loud: Lord, Thank you for your love for me; I dip myself and this room in the blood of Jesus, and I put my trust in you to deliver me from any demonic spirits that are oppressing me. Oh God, I come to you for deliverance from shame, guilt, disgust... (* insert your burden). Set me free from the power of these demonic spirits in Jesus' name.

Nighttime confession:

_____

_____

_____

_____

_____

_____

_____

_____

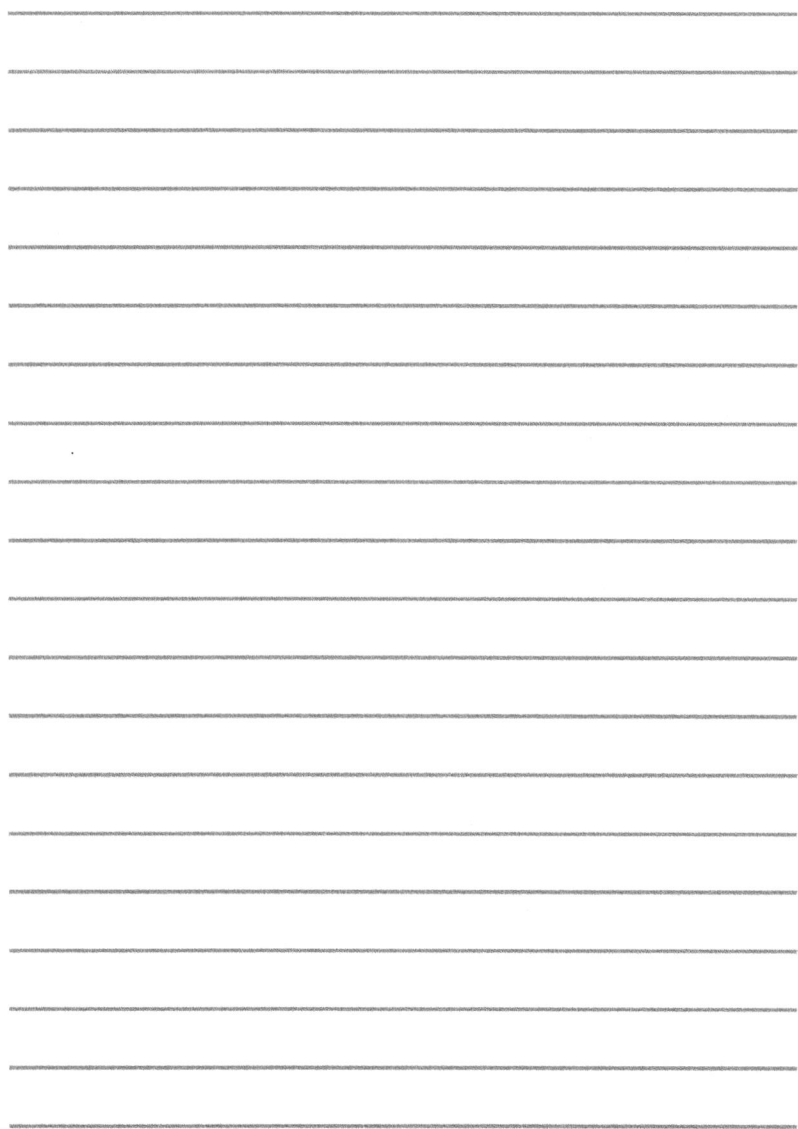

DAY 2

"Teshuvah" (The Return).

Your Return.

He who conceals his transgressions will not prosper, but whoever confesses and turns away from his sins will find compassion and mercy.
—*Proverbs 28:13 Amplified*

At the turn of the year, the season when kings go out [to battle], David sent Joab with his officers and all Israel with him, and they devastated Ammon and besieged Rabbah; David remained in Jerusalem. Late one afternoon, David rose from his couch and strolled on the roof of the royal palace; and from the roof, he saw a woman bathing. The woman was very beautiful, and the king sent someone to make inquiries about the woman. He reported, " She is Bathsheba daughter of Eliam [and] wife of Uriah the Hittite." David sent messengers to fetch her; she came to him and he lay with her - she had just purified herself after her period - and she went back home. The woman conceived, and she sent word to David, "I am pregnant." Thereupon David sent a message to Joab, " Send Uriah the Hittite to me"; and Joab sent Uriah to David 2 Samuel 11:1-6 JPS

In this passage of scripture, we see King David, a man after God's own heart, sin, consciously and willingly. The first sin was the lust of the eyes, *"and from the roof, he saw."* His eyes here preceded any actual acts of adultery, for as it is written, *"But I say to you that whoever looks at a woman to lust for her has already committed adultery with her in his heart."*- Matthew 5:28 NKJV

Now that the thought of adultery has already been planted in his mind, David acts on his flesh desire and sends a messenger to retrieve information about her. When the report comes back, he learns she is a married woman to a soldier, Uriah the Hittite. Held captive to his sinful nature of lust and fleshly desire, David sends for Bathsheba to come to the palace, and he had sex with her, fulfilling the burning passion and satisfying his flesh.

As a result of this action, a child was conceived. Now David, who was aware of his sin, continued to spiral down the wrong path instead of returning to the Lord his God to confess. Therefore, in his own might, he conspired within himself to reconcile the situation and intentionally plotted the death of Uriah the Hittite by having him assigned to the front lines to be killed. In this act of shedding innocent blood and committing murder, he fulfilled the warning of scripture as it is written in Hebrews 12:15, *"looking carefully lest anyone fall short of the grace of God; lest any root of bitterness springing up cause trouble, and by this many become defiled."*- NKJV.

Furthermore, David took it upon himself to marry Bathsheba, and they bore a son, which greatly displeased the Lord, so he sent Nathan to David.

> *Upon Nathan's arrival, he said to him, "There were two men in the same city, one rich and one poor. The rich man had very large flocks and herds, but the poor man had only one little ewe lamb that he had bought. He tended it, and it grew up together with him and his children:It used to share his morsel of bread, drink from his cup, and nestle in his bosom; it was like a daughter to him. One day, a traveler came to the rich man, but he was loath to take anything from his own flocks or herds to prepare a meal for the guest who had come to him; so, he took the poor man's lamb and prepared it for the man who had come to him." David flew into rage against the man, and said to Nathan, "As the Lord lives, the man who did this deserves to die! He shall pay for the Lamb four times over because he did such a thing and showed no pity." And Nathan said to David, " That man is you! 2nd Samuel 12:1-7*

This parable clearly depicts the acts of David with Bathsheba, and he couldn't see himself in the parable because his eyes were held captive to the lust of this world. Once another anointed man of God came to David and delivered this message, the veil was lifted enough for David to acknowledge, and he then admitted his guilt before the Lord.

In what ways have you been like David from these passages of scripture?

Have you ever lusted after men or women?

Have you stolen?

Have you cheated or committed adultery?

Have you murdered? (physically, mentally, emotionally, or spiritually)

Have you done something out of spite?

Who do you have grudges against?

List all the things that you have done below. The key is to be honest with yourself and God.

Repeat this prayer out loud: Heavenly Father, I stand guilty before You, and I invite you into this place of shame, guilt, bitterness, and fear. Send Your Holy Spirit to draw out of me all condemnation of my actions and cleanse me with the blood of my Lord and Savior Jesus Christ. I bind every spirit in me that is not of Jesus Christ and forbid them from hindering my confession and acknowledgments of my sins. In Jesus' Mighty name. Amen.

Daytime confession:

Nighttime confession.

How do you feel about yourself? Write in detail how you feel about yourself and the details of what you have done from your list earlier today. Here is an opportunity to be raw, real, naked, and unfiltered with the Holy Spirit about these things.

Repeat this prayer out loud: Holy Spirit, I invite you into this prayer time, and I ask you to heal my heart as I submit the details of how I feel about myself and the details of the things I have done. Heavenly Father, I admit that I am weak and surrender my will, mind, heart, spirit, soul, and body to you now. Deliver me from the guilt of my conscience, subconscious, and unconscious mind. In Jesus' mighty name. Amen.

_____

_____

_____

_____

_____

_____

_____

_____

_____

_____

Free Expession

DAY 3

The First Day of " Asseret Yemei HaTeshuvah"

Ten Days of Repentance

The Call to Repentance

If we confess our sin, He is faithful and just to forgive us our sins and to cleanse us from all unrighteousness. 1 John 1:9 NKJV

As you begin the first day of 10 in repentance to the Lord, be encouraged in knowing, *"for all have sinned and fall short of the glory of God, being justified freely by His grace through the redemption that is in Christ Jesus, whom God set forth as a propitiation by His blood, through faith, to demonstrate His righteousness, because in His forbearance God had passed over the sins that were previously committed, to demonstrate at the present time, His righteousness, that He might be just and the justifier of the one who has faith in Jesus."* Romans 3:23-26 NKJV

Glancing back at King David and his fall from glory, we learn that he took Uriah the Hittite's wife, Bathsheba, had sex with her, killed her husband, took her as his wife, and conceived a son.

Yet, he was still considered *"a man after God's own heart,"* and from his lineage descended the Messiah, Yeshua, "Jesus Christ of Nazareth." The nagging question is, how did David commit all these crimes against the Lord and maintain a close, unbreakable, and unshakable relationship with God?

The answer can be found in the famous prayer of repentance as it is written in Psalm 51. (Take a moment, grab your Bible, read, and highlight this prayer.)

Now that you've read it, take your pen and underline verse 3: *"For I acknowledge my transgressions, and my sin is always before me."* And verse 6: *Behold, you desire truth in the inward parts, and in the hidden part, You will make to know wisdom.*

The key in these verses is acknowledging - meaning to accept the existence or truth of your faults. Let's take a stroll back to King David, who did not immediately turn to God after his fall from glory, because as we learn in 2nd Samuel 12:14: the child about to be born was destined to die because of this sin David committed. Since the child was about to be born, and then was actually born according to 2nd Samuel 12:15: the Lord afflicted the child that

Uriah's wife had borne to David. This signifies that there was a minimum of 9 months from David laying with Bathsheba and her conceiving to the birth of their son that David did not acknowledge or "accept " his sin to himself or confess it to God. Furthermore, we now know he didn't immediately accept the truth and consequences of his sin because in 2nd Samuel 12:16 we read that, "*David entreated God for the boy; David fasted, and he went in and spent the night lying on the ground.*" In this time of lamentation (grief, sorrow, and weeping), David prays the prayer in Psalm 51, leading us to verse 6, "*You desire truth in the inward parts.*"

What this means is that with the consequences of the death of his son with Bathsheba for his reckless behavior, David's eyes were opened to the importance of turning to God, immediately accepting and confronting within himself the guilt, shame, and bloodshed from his decisions that he was blinded to during the 9-month stint of the pregnancy.

I've noticed that even in my own personal journey, accepting all the ways I've been flat out in rebellion against God, willingly and in a conscious mind, and accepting the truth within myself and confessing out loud these things have been incredibly difficult and seemingly impossible.

Guilt, shame, blame, pain, condemnation, and fear all crept inside and made me feel like I'm just a bad person. I felt like God would never forgive me, or I was flooded with the thoughts that I was too deep into my sin, so what's the point in going to God? He sees what I've been doing, so I don't need to say it.

However, what I've learned was that all these thoughts and feelings were manipulations by demons that wanted to keep me bound, blind, and confused about the reconciliation power through the blood of Jesus.

What are you hiding deep within? Write down your deepest darkest secrets and read them out loud to yourself and the Holy Spirit.

"with the mouth confession is made unto salvation"
Romans 10:10 NKJV

Pray this prayer out loud: Heavenly Father, I request and petition you for an innumerable amount of angels of war to assist me in this battle. Holy Spirit, I believe in my heart and confess with my heart that Jesus Christ is Lord, and I trade in my transgressions for His righteousness and receive the reconciliation to You through the powerful blood of Jesus.

Daytime confession:

Are you mad at God?

The foolishness of man ruins his way, And his heart rages against the Lord. - Proverbs 19:3 NSAB1995

It's okay to be angry and upset with God about what you've endured in your life. It's about what you do with that anger that leads you down a path of foolishness or healing. Telling Jesus Christ that you're mad at him and inviting Him into the pain is the path to healing.

Write below: Holy Spirit, I invite you into this prayer time, and I cover this prayer with the blood of Jesus. Jesus, I'm pissed off .... (Let it flow, and give it all to Him.)

Nighttime confession:

_____

_____

_____

_____

_____

_____

_____

_____

_____

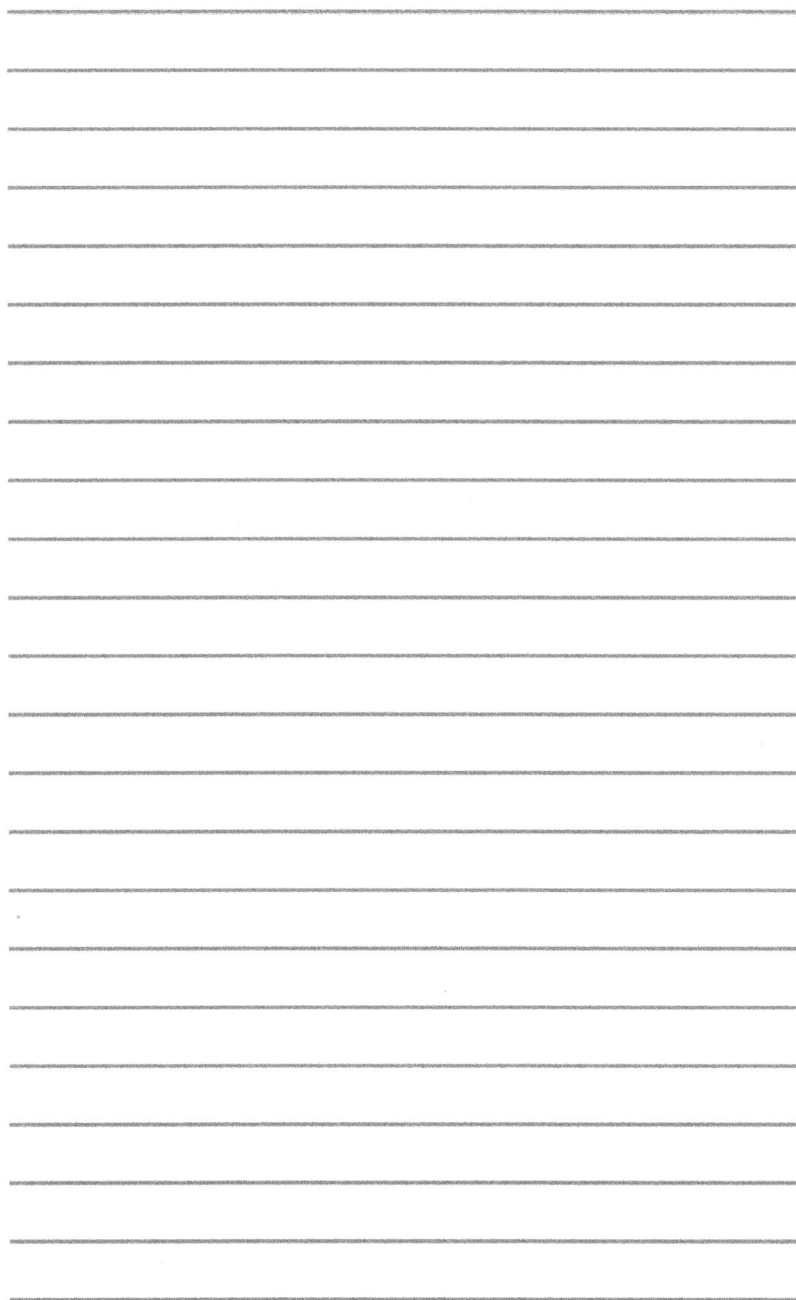

DAY 4

The 2nd Day of Repentance

Tearing Down "idols"

Then Samuel spoke to all the house of Israel, saying, "If you return to the LORD with all your hearts, then put away the foreign gods and the Ashtoreths from among you, and prepare your hearts for the LORD, and serve Him only; and He will deliver you from the hand of the Philistines. 1 Samuel 7:3 NKJV

Turning back to the Lord requires tearing down ALL the love, admiration, reverence, images, and representation of people, things, and desires that have taken place of the One True Living God in your life.

In today's scripture, we are examining the prophet and last judge, Samuel's judgment of Israel. As we read this, we must also keep at the forefront of our minds that, *"For there is no distinction between Jew and Greek, for the same Lord over all is rich to all who call upon Him."* Romans 10:12. NKJV

It is important to know that in your spirit, soul, and body, you are called to the Lord in the same way that the Israelites from this scripture, and Jews today, are called to come back to the Lord in repentance.

The house of Israel had turned their backs away from God and got themselves caught up in an assortment of different gods and specifically in the goddess of lust, which is representative of Ashtoreth. In current times, we - as people of God - are not much different from the cycle of disobedience and rebellion against God that the Israelites went through. An example of a modern-day, foreign god includes celebrities that we follow, sing the songs of, join fan clubs, etc. They have taken the place of the praise, worship, love, and exhortation of the Most High God.

Another form of idolization today is social media and the hours and hours we spend on it daily. This greatly exceeds the amount of time we spend reading the Word of God, meditating on the word of God, and worshiping God. Furthermore, the world we live in is a breeding ground and training camp for lust, which is often confused with love. We seek picture-perfect relationships displayed publicly for all to see, while at the same time, being timid or ashamed of publicly professing the name of Jesus Christ as Lord and Savior.

In order to put down false gods and immorality of all sorts, you must first admit verbally to the Lord that you have idols in your life. Next, you must shift away from these idols, which will come in the form of unfollowing people, changing the music you listen to, changing the shows you watch, switching up your friends and family, and decreasing your social media time. Action must follow the confession, which will be a slow process of letting these things go. If your heart desires the Lord, open your mouth and invite the Holy Spirit into this space with you, and He will begin to deliver you.

What idols do you have in your life? How much time do you spend on social media vs. the Word of God? What TV show have you not missed a single episode of?

Pray this prayer out loud:
I release the Holy Ghost, electrical cardioversion, into my heart, and I receive the restoration of my heart back to You, Heavenly Father. In Jesus' Mighty name. Amen.

Day time confession:

What images do you have in your mind about your life? Relationship partner? Money? Material things?

How much time do you spend planning to obtain these things vs. the things of God?

Nighttime confession:

_____

_____

_____

_____

_____

_____

_____

_____

_____

_____

_____

_____

_____

_____

_____

_____

DAY 5

"Rend Your Heart"

3rd Day of Repentance

"Now, therefore," says the LORD, "Turn to Me with all your heart, With fasting, with weeping, and with mourning." Joel 2:12 NKJV

When you return to the Lord, He is gracious and merciful.

Answering the call of repentance is a process. And in that process, you will find yourself ugly-crying and snotting as you release your mistakes, pain, frustration, worries, and anxieties on the Lord.

Giving your heart to the Lord will come with a great deal of emotional pain in the beginning. Why? Genesis 6:3 can give us some insight, as it is written, *"Then the LORD said, "My Spirit shall not strive and remain with man forever, because he is indeed flesh [sinful, corrupt—given over to sensual appetites]; nevertheless, his days shall yet be a hundred and twenty years." - AMP*

The part that stands out here is "*he is indeed flesh [sinful, corrupt]*" because we are born into sin, and we have to make a concise choice to connect with God, which goes against our natural sinful nature. Once we make the choice and take the action to open our mouths and say, "Heavenly Father, I am a sinner" and verbalize our specific sins, we activate our free will. Our will is contained in our soul, and the soul needs to be in an afflicted state to the Lord in surrender to His majesty. It is in this place of weeping, sorrow, and brokenness that He is made strong, which allows Him to extract out of you all the things of this world that have made life difficult for you.

I use my life as an example of a world teaching that made my life difficult - premarital sex - I had sex out of wedlock, like the majority of the population. And in this sin, I encountered several challenges, such as receiving the spirit of comparison. Sexually, I found myself trying to find value in performance in the act, and when that did not yield, the results that were promised to me by the world's standards (to give me my hearts desires), I found myself depressed and believing that I was valueless in a relationship - all of which were lies and manipulation by the enemy.

How I discovered that this was a lie came with fasting. I began a Daniel fast for 7 days in a simulation of Daniel 10:2-3: "*In those days I, Daniel, was mourning three full weeks. I ate no pleasant food, no meat or wine came into my mouth, nor did I anoint myself at all, till three whole weeks were fulfilled."* In doing so, I was acting on my choice to surrender to the Lord's will for my life. And in that fast and weeping, he began to purge my pains of my decisions by changing my heart.

Over the next 3 days, do a Daniel fast. What fears do you have about the Lord God and his acceptance of you?

Pray this prayer out loud: Heavenly Father, I come to the Throne of Mercy, confessing I am weak; and I surrender my own self-defense tactics and weapons to You, in the name of Jesus.

Daytime confession:

_____

_____

_____

_____

_____

_____

_____

_____

_____

_____

_____

What things from your past or present have been on your mind all day?

Pray this prayer out loud:
I renounce all agreements known and unknown that I have made through the sin in my life in the name of Jesus.

Nighttime confession:

DAY 6

Intercession

Sealed with the Promise of the Holy Spirit

"The people came to Moses and said, "We have sinned, because we have spoken against the Lord and you; intercede with the Lord, that He may remove the serpents from us." And Moses interceded for the people."
Numbers 21:7JPS

As a servant of the Most High God, I am charged to intercede on your behalf under the command of the ultimate Intercessor to all who believe, Jesus Christ of Nazareth.

On this 4th Day of repentance, I come to the throne room in the presence of You, Heavenly Father, our Lord and Savior Jesus Christ, and You, Holy Spirit, to submit the case of the person writing to you in this journal in the name of Jesus.

Heavenly Father, I stand by the side of the one confessing to you in this journal and request that You release your Holy Spirit to draw them near them and closer to you, piercing through bone and marrow to separate spirit and soul of this person and sealing them with the promises of the Holy Spirit in Jesus' name.

Today's challenge has been on your mind, time, and attention. You may have noticed that you are more irritated, frustrated, angry, low energy, restless, have a hard time concentrating, fatigued, and distracted - just to name a few moods. If you are experiencing this, be encouraged as this is a sign that you are co-laboring with the Lord in the battle for your soul and the reconciliation of your heart, mind, and body to Him who cares for you and has given you eternal life.

Pushing through all those feelings, frustrations, and thoughts that you don't feel like completing this section today is the true test of your faith in Him who has come to set you free.

What emotions have you been feeling the last few days? What hurts from your past or present have resurfaced in your thoughts?

Pray this prayer out loud: Heavenly Father, I submit my will, mind, body, soul, and spirit to you for examination in the name of Jesus.

Daytime confession:

What happened today that upset you? What challenges have you had in completing today's confession?

Nighttime confession:

_____

_____

_____

_____

_____

_____

_____

_____

_____

_____

_____

_____

_____

_____

_____

_____

DAY 7

Lamentation

Create in Me a New Heart

Now while Ezra was praying and making confession, weeping and prostrating himself before the house of God, a very large assembly, men, women and children, gathered to him from Israel; for the people wept bitterly. Ezra 10:1 JPS

Shedding tears in Godly sorrow while admitting to Jesus your participation in sexual immorality, stealing, lying, betrayal, manipulation, backbiting, slander, rebellion, and disobedience is a living sacrifice that is sweet in the eyes of the Lord.

The greatest battle you will face in these 40 days and nights will be against guilt, shame, and blame. However, I remind you that, *"There is therefore now no condemnation to those who are in Christ Jesus, who do not walk according to the flesh, but according to the Spirit."* - Romans 8:1 NKJV

As Ezra and the people of Israel shed ugly tears for their trespasses against God, so shall you experience this as you surrender to the Lord Our God. A common misconception is that tears and ugly crying on the floor to God is a bad thing; however, this is the exact space in which you experience the greatest manifestation and answers to your prayers.

By now, you should have experienced some tears shed; you may even be holding back tears throughout the day as the Lord is ministering and releasing His grace, mercy, and forgiveness over you on this 5th Day of repentance. Be encouraged as this is the love of the Father, so, *"Trust in the LORD with all your heart, and lean not on your own understanding; In all your ways acknowledge Him, and He shall direct your paths."* - Proverbs 3:5-6 NKJV

What have you done that you're ashamed, guilty, or embarrassed by?

Pray this out loud: I renounce all murderous thoughts, idolatrous words I have spoken, sorcery, divination, and occult involvement in the past or the present in the name of Jesus.

Daytime confession:

What has been done to you by others that has caused you to feel ashamed, embarrassed, humiliated, devalued, or devastated? Who did this to you? How do you feel about them? How do you feel about yourself?

Pray this out loud: I release myself from the shackles of shame, embarrassment, humiliation, devaluation, and devastation, and I declare that I am set free by Jesus Christ.

Nighttime Confession:

_____

_____

_____

_____

_____

_____

_____

_____

_____

_____

_____

_____

_____

DAY 8

Atonement

Broken and Contrite Spirit

For any person who is not afflicted in soul on that same day shall be cut off from his people. And any person who does any work on that same day, that person I will destroy from among his people. Leviticus 23:29 NKJV

Stress, weakness, overwhelming emotional pain, suffocating circumstances, and heartbreak are just a few of the many afflicted states of the soul. I am sure that at some point in your life you've experienced one of these states.

In this scripture, God gives us a clear direction on what is required for atonement. Now we have to go further and tie in that atonement. In this scriptural, Era looked a little different because Jesus Christ had not yet come in the flesh; therefore, the sacrifice required was a broken and contrite heart and blood of an unblemished animal.

The blood is significant because it's the only thing that atones for the sin of man. However, it's important to note that Hebrews 9:18 states, *"Therefore not even the first covenant was dedicated without blood because the way to fellowship with God is through blood in reconciliation to our Heavenly Father.*

Moreover, making the new covenant, *"Then Jesus said to them, "Most assuredly, I say to you, unless you eat the flesh of the Son of Man and drink His blood, you have no life in you. Whoever eats My flesh and drinks My blood has eternal life, and I will raise him up at the last day. For My flesh is food indeed, and My blood is drink indeed. He who eats My flesh and drinks My blood abides in Me, and I in him." John 6:53-56*

Blood is the most powerful covenant to be covered by because as it is written, *"but with the precious blood of Christ, as of a lamb without blemish and without spot. He indeed was foreordained before the foundation of the world, but was manifest in these last times for you who through Him believe in God, who raised Him from the dead and gave Him glory, so that your faith and hope are in God."*

This sacrifice was done as the ultimate payment for any and all sins, from murder, rape, lying, stealing, sexual immorality, rebellion, disobedience, and all other sins which are unholy and unacceptable in His sight. And all you have to do is activate the power of the blood of Jesus in admitting your faults to the Lord in the name of Jesus. Your verbal confessions of these things, daily, allow the blood of the Lamp to purge you and wash you so you can be white as snow. In doing this daily, your faith will grow by exercising your confidence in the redemptive power of the blood of Jesus and the sealing of the promises of the Holy Spirit.

What, in your life, has repeatedly played on your mind repeatedly or that you haven't gotten over?

Say this prayer out loud:

Lord Jesus, I believe that you are the Way, the Truth, and the Life, and there is no other way to fellowship with the Father except through you. Therefore I submit my soul to you and confess that I am weak, brokenhearted, devastated, stressed, overwhelmed, scared, ashamed, and guilty of sin, and I invite You, Holy Spirit, into this area of affliction in my soul - to restore it back to you in Jesus' mighty name. Amen.

Daytime confession:

_____

_____

_____

_____

_____

_____

_____

_____

What are the deepest, darkest pains of your entire life?

Nighttime confession:

_____

_____

_____

_____

_____

_____

_____

_____

_____

_____

_____

_____

_____

_____

_____

_____

_____

_____

_____

_____

_____

DAY 9

Repentance

You Desire Truth in the Inward Parts

It shall be to you a sabbath of solemn rest, and you shall afflict your souls; on the ninth day of the month at evening, from evening to evening, you shall celebrate your sabbath." Leviticus 23:32 NKJV

Today is the day to log out of social media, refrain from turning on the TV, limit incoming or outside personal calls and text messages, and simply dwell in the presence of the Lord.

Use today as a day of praise and worship of the Most High God. Play your favorite gospel songs - singing along, dancing, and ushering in the Holy Spirit.

From the time you wake up to the time that you go to sleep, your challenge is to keep your eyes focused on the Lord in songs of praises and the reading of His Word. Visit this passage and read the whole chapter. Leviticus 23:1-44

What songs of praise are on your mind right now? What do you want God to change in your life as you sing these songs today?

Daytime confession:

_____

_____

_____

_____

_____

_____

_____

_____

_____

_____

_____

_____

_____

_____

_____

_____

_____

What did you feel or experience as you worshiped today? What struggles did you have with staying off of social media, RV, and limiting personal calls?

Nighttime Confession:

_____

_____

_____

_____

_____

_____

_____

_____

_____

_____

_____

_____

_____

_____

_____

_____

DAY 10

Yod [completion]

Godly Sorrow Produces Repentance

If My people who are called by My name will humble themselves, and pray and seek My face, and turn from their wicked ways, then I will hear from heaven and will forgive their sin and heal their land. 2 chronicles 7:14 NKJV

God is not a man that He should lie! Therefore, His urgent call for your repentance is so precious to Him that, *"He will make an everlasting covenant with them, that I will not turn away from doing them good; but I will put My fear in their hearts so that they will not depart from Me. Yes, I will rejoice over them to do them good, and I will assuredly plant them in this land, with all My heart and with all My soul."* - Jeremiah 32:40 NKJV

Furthermore, says the LORD, *"I will put My laws in their mind and write them on their hearts; and I will be their God, and they shall be My people. None of them shall teach his neighbor, and none his brother, saying,*

'Know the LORD,' for all shall know Me, from the least of them to the greatest of them. For I will be merciful to their unrighteousness, and their sins and their lawless deeds I will remember no more." Hebrews 8:10-13 NKJV

You have to do your part to bow down in the presence of the Lord and accept the new covenant by way of Jesus Christ. Walking after the Lord, keeping His commands, His Testimonies, and His statutes with all your heart and soul. You accomplish this by opening your mouth and speaking The Word of God with your admission of wrongdoing, daily, and He will hear you and forgive you, according to His tender mercies.

What is weighing you down mentally, emotionally and spiritually today?

Daytime confession:

_____

_____

_____

_____

_____

_____

_____

What fears, hesitations, or questions do you have concerning the Lord's forgiveness of your mistakes from the past or present?

Nighttime confession:

_____

_____

_____

_____

_____

_____

_____

_____

_____

_____

_____

_____

_____

_____

_____

_____

_____

_____

DAY 11

Holy Spirit Draws

He is Close to Those Who Are Brokenhearted

He heals the brokenhearted and binds up their wounds.
Psalms 147:3 NKJV

In the world, we are taught that brokenness is a weakness that will lead you to be trampled all over. And if you show any signs of it, especially to those who have contributed to that state you become a doormat in their eyes.

On the contrary, we learn in the Holy Scriptures that God works best in those who are shattered, desperate for Him, and what we would call 'underdogs,' and in that, He is made strong.

Think about this: Jesus, our Lord and Savior, came in the flesh and lived among us. In His time among us, He experienced every heartache, emotional, physical, and spiritual pain that can be afflicted onto the human body and soul. His own family ridiculed and did not believe Him. He was betrayed by Judas Iscariot, who was in His close circle. He was rejected by the world. He was beaten and bruised physically. He was mocked and slandered to the point of the assassination of His character. And He was persecuted unjustly.

He, as our Savior, guide, and master, had to become chiseled down to a state of brokenness in body, soul, and Spirit in order to manifest the unlimited power of the Heavenly Father in which we have received the greatest gift of eternal life through the resurrection of Jesus Christ - who rose on the third day, conquering death, giving us back our full inheritance of salvation, and earning us a seat next to Him at the right hand of God.

In this journey, you will need to work by renewing your mind with The Word in order to shift your idea of what it means to be broken. When you learn this and continuously profess your brokenness to the Lord, you exalt Him - acknowledging that His ways are above our ways, which leads to submission.

Can you admit to yourself and God that you are broken? If you answer yes, how are you broken? If no, why not?

Say this prayer out loud: This year, fear will have no part in me, in the name of Jesus.

Daytime Confession:

_____

_____

_____

_____

_____

_____

_____

_____

_____

_____

_____

_____

_____

_____

_____

_____

_____

_____

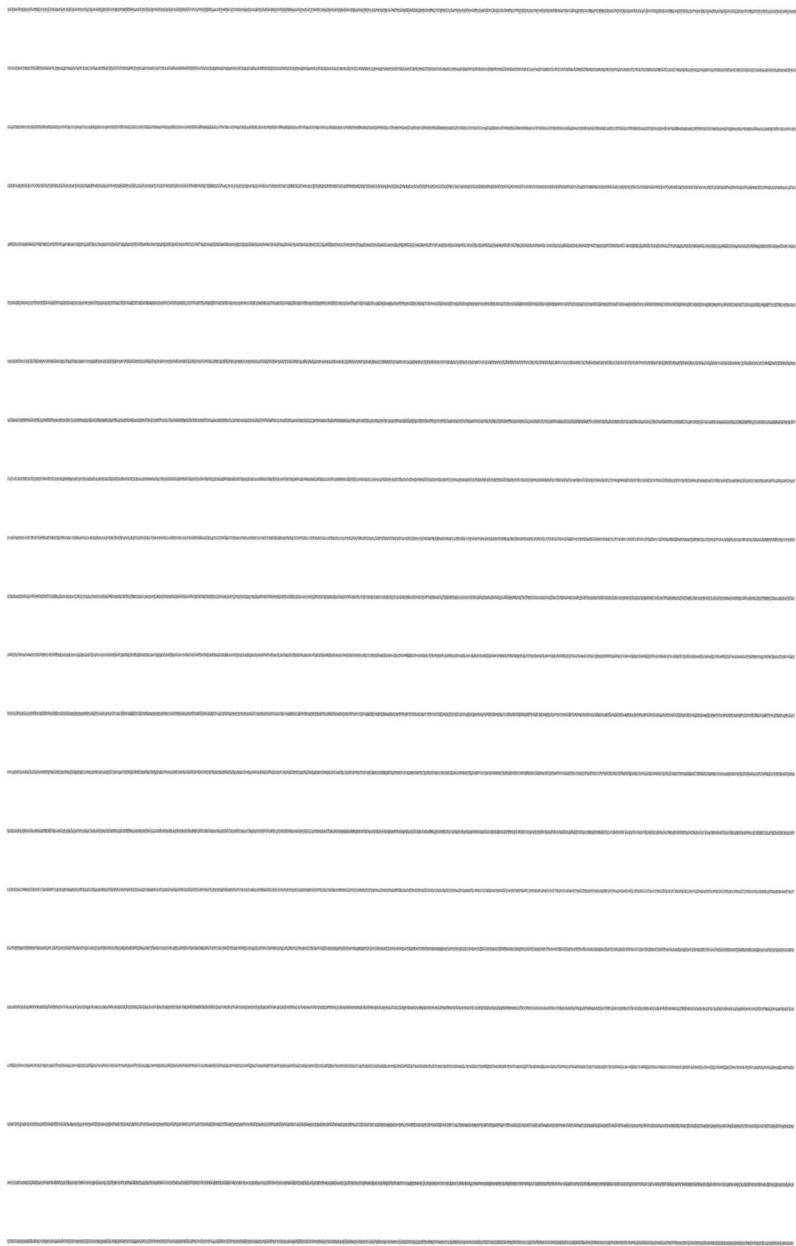

When was the last time you were hanging on by a thread – mentally, emotionally, and spiritually? What type of feelings did that come with?

_____

_____

_____

_____

_____

_____

_____

_____

_____

_____

_____

_____

_____

_____

_____

_____

_____

_____

_____

_____

DAY 12

I Am the First and the Last

Lord all my Desire is before You

And you shall love the LORD your God with all your heart, with all your soul, with all your mind, and with all your strength.' This is the first commandment. Mark 13:30 NKJV

Loving the Lord your God with all your heart is challenging. When we think of the word "all" in our natural world brain logic, it's hard for us to fathom giving the whole amount of our hearts to God. Naturally, we tend to keep some part of us back as a fail-safe plan in the event that God disappoints us.

I want to bring your attention to the story of Ananias and Sapphira (Acts 5), in which we have a depiction of what we do when it comes to reserving a portion to ourselves instead of giving our all. In this passage, the price for not giving all to God is high.

As it is written, *"But a certain man named Ananias, with Sapphira his wife, sold a possession. And he kept back part of the proceeds, his wife also being aware of it, and brought a certain part and laid it at the apostles' feet. But Peter said, "Ananias, why has Satan filled your heart to lie to the Holy Spirit and keep back part of the price of the land for yourself? While it remained, was it not your own? And after it was sold, was it not in your own control? Why have you conceived this thing in your heart? You have not lied to men but to God." Then Ananias, hearing these words, fell down and breathed his last. So great fear came upon all those who heard these things."*

In connecting to scriptural texts, a mystery and a revelation are revealed to us. When we conceive in our hearts, minds, and souls to hold back even a small portion from God, we are operating in our own strength as if we are bigger than God in some way - and we are not.

> *"For the wages of sin is death, but the gift of God is eternal life in Christ Jesus our Lord." - Romans 6:23 NKJV.*

Therefore, any self-preservation in love, heart, mind, soul, and strength, much like Ananias and later Sapphira from the text, leads to death.

What have you kept back from the Lord?

Pray this prayer out loud: Heavenly Father, I come to the Throne of Mercy to submit my spirit, soul, body, heart and mind to you for examination. I surrender all self-righteousness known and unknown in my life, and I ask you to change me, O God, and make me more like you in this area of my life. In Jesus' Mighty name. Amen.

Daytime Confession:

_____

_____

_____

_____

_____

_____

_____

_____

_____

_____

_____

_____

_____

_____

_____

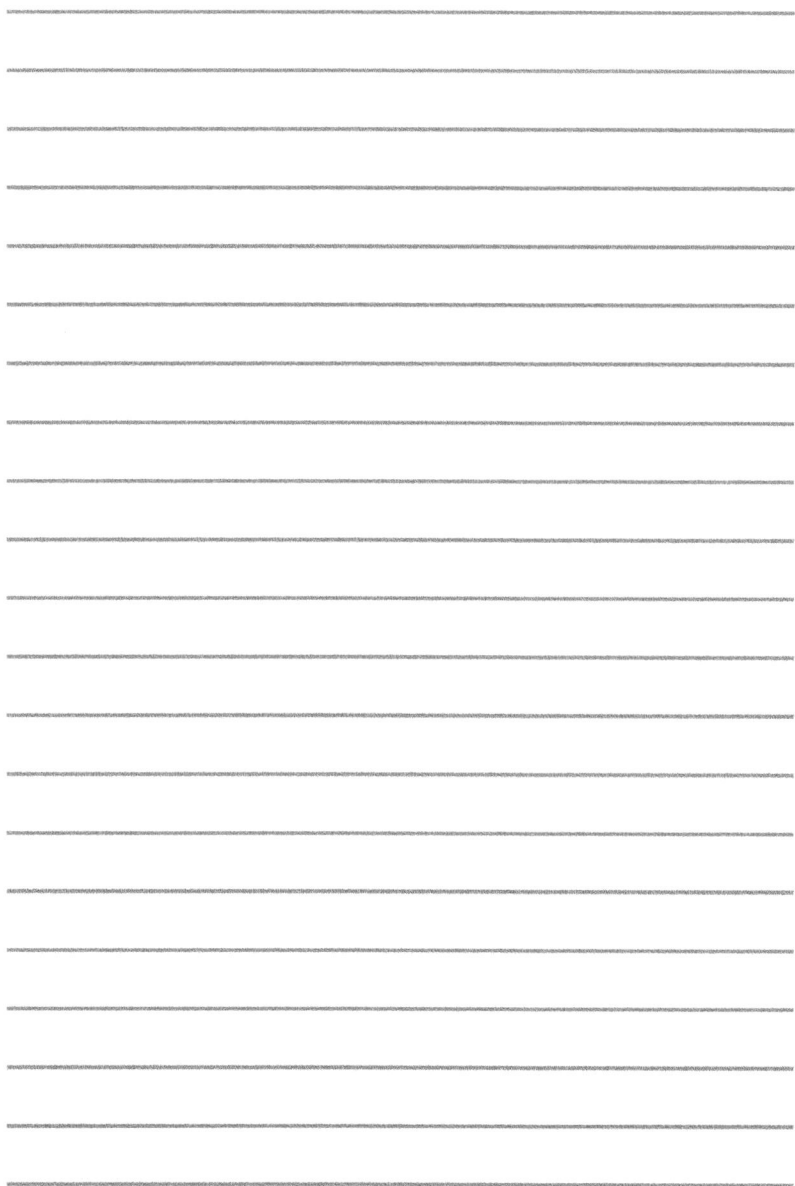

Why are you afraid to trust the Lord with all of your mess?

Nighttime confession:

_____

_____

_____

_____

_____

_____

_____

_____

_____

_____

_____

_____

_____

_____

_____

_____

_____

_____

_____

DAY 13

I Am the Resurrection and the Life

Nothing is Impossible for God

Now a certain woman had a flow of blood for twelve years, and had suffered many things from many physicians. She had spent all that she had and was no better, but rather grew worse Mark 5:25 NKJV

Bishop Sapp said it best:

1. Selfcare: attending to and respecting the limitations and needs *that God has designed for you. You know how much you can handle*, so don't go past what you can't handle.

2. Self-ish care: has become the norm. Doing things we want (for no purpose other than to have our own way), not taking into account who is around, how people are going to feel about it, as long as I benefit, and how it affects or infects that person.

3. Soul care: learning to live our life with God. I'm not just saved, but I understand that there is a life God wants me to experience. My life as a believer is not boring; I'm not regulated by rules; there are things I don't do anymore; I'm free because whosoever the Son has set free is free indeed.

The difference between these three (and being honest about where you fall) is key in identifying WHY you're overwhelmed with your life.

Mark 5:25-34 is the best example of this. In short, it's about a woman with the issue of blood for 12 years.

Diving deeper, we read in Mark 5:26, "*And had suffered many things of many physicians, and had spent all that she had, and was nothing bettered, but rather grew worse.*"

Additionally, this woman had physical, emotional, and physiological damage from her situation. For years, she was not capable of being a wife, mother, friend, daughter, cousin, or niece.

In fact, she was not able to fulfill these roles, and she even had a "self-care routine." Our text says she *"suffered many things of many physicians,"* meaning she sought and had clinical, professional, licensed, and medical help from scholars, experts, and accredited professionals in the fields of many things. She suffered, YET, she was broken - still damaged emotionally, physically, and psychologically, and her condition GREW WORSE.

Why? The most obvious answer is that there was no mention prior to verse 27, in which SHE CHOSE or TURNED TO GOD. Meaning, she had *exhausted all of her options in her own strength to handle something ONLY JESUS CHRIST can heal and deliver.* Miraculously, when she heard of Jesus, realizing she had not tried Him, she touched the hem of his garment, and immediately she was healed.

When will you change your strategy?

Daytime Confession:

_____

_____

_____

_____

_____

_____

_____

_____

_____

_____

What strategies have you tried outside of God? What was the result of executing these strategies?

Nighttime confession?

DAY 14

I Am the Alpha and the Omega

Rise, take up your bed and walk

Now a certain man was there who had an infirmity thirty-eight years. When Jesus saw him lying there and knew that he already had been in that condition a long time, He said to him, "Do you want to be made well?" John 5:5

I love this story because it is a very vivid and relatable reminder that Jesus will still heal you no matter how much time has passed in your suffering.

This man that Jesus met at the pool of Bethesda spent over two and a half decades in a "sick condition." I remind you that Jesus said, *"Those who are well have no need of a physician, but those who are sick. I did not come to call the righteous, but sinners, to repentance."* - Mark 2:17 NKJV. He refers to the sick who need a doctor's care, and He is the ultimate doctor who can and has healed all manners of sickness.

The key to this healing is FAITH and BELIEF. However, a lot of us tend to respond in the same manner as the man in this passage. *"The sick man answered Him, "Sir, I have no man to put me into the pool when the water is stirred up; but while I am coming, another steps down before me."* John 5:7 NKJV. We leave our faith in that spot of an excuse of why we haven't been able to be healed. And that's a dangerous place to be because we then give room for doubt and unbelief to be manipulated - so we do not see the full manifestation of the healing power of Jesus Christ.

In this journey, the Holy Spirit is asking you, "Do you want to be made well?" I encourage you to activate your faith, no matter how many years have gone by. And when you start to feel helpless and hopeless, revisit this passage and remember that this man suffered for 38 years, and he still was made fully well - immediately. If Jesus can do it for him, He can do it for you. *"Therefore, I say to you, whatever things you ask when you pray, believe that you receive them, and you will have them."* Mark 11:24 NKJV

What have you been suffering from mentally, emotionally, physically, and spiritually? How many years have you been suffering?

Pray this prayer out loud: Holy Spirit, I invite you into the sicknesses deep within my heart, mind, body, and soul, and I receive my healing because by His stripes I am healed. In Jesus' Mighty name.

Daytime confession:

_____

_____

_____

_____

_____

_____

_____

_____

_____

_____

_____

_____

_____

What is at the root of your sickness? Rejection, bitterness, persecution, abandonment, neglect, abuse, etc.?

Nighttime confession:

_____

_____

_____

_____

_____

_____

_____

_____

_____

_____

_____

_____

_____

_____

_____

_____

_____

_____

DAY 15

Authority

Even the unclean spirits obey

And when He stepped out on the land, there met Him, a certain man from the city who had demons for a long time. Luke 8:27

The church has failed in teaching us that demons are more than just a symbol of evil. Due to this lack of teaching, *" My people are destroyed for lack of knowledge." Hosea 4:6 NKJV*

However, the good news is found in the gospel in which we are witnessing God pouring out His Spirit and re-teaching His Word through willing vessels in the last days.

On this day by the blood of Jesus, we shatter and melt all blinders and veils of darkness over our eyes and see The Truth. Demons are more than symbols of evil, they are real beings that *"come except to steal, and to kill, and to destroy." John 10:10 NKJV*

These beings are spirits because God is a spirit, and they can enter into the physical body of a person much as they did with the man in this passage. This man from the text had demons for years, and in those years, they influenced the man's life. They had him doing all kinds of things, such as walking around naked everywhere he went and living in places where the dead reside.

Therefore, we learn that demons influence and manipulate people's behaviors. Now, to bring this into practical application, think of a specific behavior in your life that you have struggled with for years. For example, sex, drug use, lying, stealing, fighting, anger issues, mental issues, emotional issues, etc. Now think about everything you've done to try and stop this behavior. When you've relapsed back into that sin, have you felt like there is just something that keeps you stuck in that behavior, no matter what you try?

In several cases, this is not a matter of you not being able to kick a habit. Like the man in this passage, you have to face the reality that this could be a demon that is influencing this behavior. Furthermore, if this is the case, you will need to come to the knowledge that the demon is inside of you.

As you continue in the process of submitting to Jesus, Jesus will look and see and if you have demons in you. They will cry out and start to cause all kinds of physical sensations in your body.

As you read The Word and the message of the day, what type of body reactions did you feel? Increased heart rate, sweating, shortness of breath, extreme exhaustion, pressure on your chest, pressure on your throat, anger, tingling or any kind, headache?

Say this prayer out loud: I bind, with the 7 chains of fire, every demon spirit and agent of Satan that has entered my body. And I release The Word of the Lord, which is active and alive and sharper than any two-edged sword to separate me and the demons in me. In doing so, I renounce all agreements that I have made with Satan and his kingdom giving these demons in my body legal grounds into my life. In the name of Jesus.

Daytime confession:

_____

_____

_____

_____

_____

_____

_____

_____

_____

What do you want to do about the demons inside of you? If nothing, why not?

Nighttime Confession:

_____

_____

_____

_____

_____

_____

_____

_____

_____

_____

_____

_____

_____

_____

_____

_____

DAY 16

Extraordinary Faith

Faith as a Mustard Seed

For a woman whose young daughter had an unclean spirit heard about Him, and she came and fell at His feet. Mark 7:25 NKJV

An Admission that there are unclean spirits in your life requires humility and desperation.

A lot of times, this type of desperation doesn't occur until we've reached a certain threshold of brokenness in which we have tried everything that we know to try, and in doing so, have gotten so tired and whipped that we fall at the feet of Jesus in weeping, pain, and helplessness.

Unclean spirits bring destruction, chaos, devastation, frustration, and emptiness to your life. If you are experiencing these things mentally, emotionally, financially, spiritually, and in relationships, it's a physical sign that there are some unclean spirits twisting and manipulating circumstances to keep you bound in the problems.

Additionally, these unclean spirits will continue to distort and manipulate your life until you die or give up desiring better for your life and children's lives. The good news is that there is a solution that has already been given to you in the form of authority. As it is written, "*Behold I have seen Satan fall from heaven like lightning. Behold I have given you AUTHORITY to trample over snakes and scorpions and to overcome all the power of darkness nothing by any means shall harm you.*"

What situations in your life have you desperate for solutions?

Pray this prayer out loud:

Lord Jesus, you said to cast all my cares, worries, and anxieties onto you. Therefore, I come to Your feet to cast my fear of unclean spirits in and around me. I bind the spirits of fear and intimidation that have kept me bound from coming to you, and I ask you, Holy Spirit, to renew in me the spirit of love, power, and a sound mind in Jesus' name. Amen.

Daytime confession:

What situations in your life have you already given up on and accepted as not able to be fixed?

Nighttime Confession:

_____

_____

_____

_____

_____

_____

_____

_____

_____

_____

_____

_____

_____

_____

_____

_____

_____

_____

DAY 17

Anoint Your Head With Oil

With My holy oil I have anointed him

A certain woman of the wives of the sons of the prophets cried out to Elisha, saying, "Your servant my husband is dead, and you know that your servant feared the LORD. And the creditor is coming to take my two sons to be his slaves."-2 Kings 4:1-7 NKJV

Elisha and the widow's oil is a great depiction of what it looks like when you are looking at your situation and feel that you have nothing - or scraps that don't seem to be enough to make something out of.

Here is a woman who comes to the man of God, Elisha, in desperation. Her desperation has her so distressed because her bill collector is coming to take her male children to work off the debt that she was left to pay after her husband died.

In her panic and stress, the man of God asked her what she has in her house and she states, *"Your maidservant has nothing in the house but a jar of oil."* 2 Kings 4:2

Let's examine this a little further. The statement, "she has nothing," was not correct. In fact, this was a lie that she came to believe in her panic, manipulated by the enemy. The Truth was that she owed a debt due to her husband's death. The seed that was planted in her mind about having nothing was done by manipulating the creditor's authority to collect the debt by intimidation and fear. We know intimidation and fear are factors because she states, *"and the creditor is coming to TAKE my two sons as slaves."*

The children in her statement automatically become subject to bondage and captivity through the acts of the parents. And when fear of man crept in, the fear of the Lord triumphed and confirmed His word in Acts 16:31: *"Believe in the Lord Jesus Christ, and you will be saved, you and your household."*

The widow's husband believed and feared the Lord, and because of this, the household was already saved. Fear of her children being taken into bondage blinded her from this promise, so she didn't see the value of what she did have - a jar of oil.

In this era, not everyone had oil or access to oil in their homes. Oil was a high commodity, and possessing it gave you an advantage in society. Therefore, because access to oil in this time was not a privilege, the fact that the widow had a jar, made the little that she did have, valuable beyond what she could even recognize. God uses oil numerous times in the Bible to anoint the heads of His people, and their heads are never in lack of it because He is their God.

Once the widow followed the guidance of the prophet Elisha, she borrowed empty jars from everyone she knew, went home with her sons, and closed the door behind her in the secret place of God. He made Himself manifest, and every jar she had collected was made full from the little that she had because nothing is impossible for God.

The moral of this lesson is that in your desperation, fearing the Lord - more than anything that has been taken or threatened to be taken - will manifest His Glory in your situation, turning what you see as nothing into something.

What has happened in your life that has left you with nothing?

Pray this prayer out loud: I reject the lies of Satan and his kingdom that have been planted in my thoughts, mind, body, and soul, and I receive the promises of the Holy Spirit and declare that my head shall never lack oil. In Jesus' name.

Daytime Confession:

Do you believe that there is something inside of you that the Lord can use? If so, what do you have?

Nighttime confession:

DAY 18

I Am Who I Am

"I have the keys of Hades and of Death"

Nebuchadnezzar spoke, saying to them, "Is it true, Shadrach, Meshach, and Abed-Nego, that you do not serve my gods or worship the gold image which I have set up? —Daniel 3:14

The message of Shadrach, Meshach, and Abed-Nego is one of my favorites in Daniel. Why? Because faithfulness to God and His faithfulness back is on full display.

The Chaldeans accuse the three men and bring them before Nebuchadnezzar. Blood hungry, they reported "facts" so punishment could be dished out for breaking faithfulness to their king. Like ravenous dogs, they barked and threw the king's own decree back in his face to provoke him to toss these men in the fiery furnace.

The response to the accusations is EVERYTHING!

Shadrach, Meshach, and Abed-Nego answered and said to the king, *"O Nebuchadnezzar, we have no need to answer you in this matter. Daniel 3:16*

(Despite the "fact" they DID NOT worship his golden image.)

Full of fury, after the response of the three men, the "king" commanded the furnace be heated seven times more than the normal heated rate, and the ravenous dogs jumped for joy, waiting for them to lose their lives.

The strongest men they could find were commanded to bind (tie together or confine with a cord or anything flexible; to fasten as with a band, filet or ligature.) the men and cast *"forcefully throw them into the furnace."*

However, on the way to the furnace, *"the flame of the fire killed those men who took up Shadrach, Meshach, and Abed-Nego." Daniel 3:22*

Bound, the men fell into the furnace, and witnesses saw four men in the fire. Confused, the question was asked, "Weren't three men cast into the fire?" The answers confirmed that yes, there were only three thrown into the fire, yet four FREED men appeared in the midst of the fire - and they are not hurt.

I LOVE this - because, in everyday life, Chaldeans, ravenous dogs, and wicked-hearted people foam at the mouth to accuse and point out how you have messed up, disobeyed, and have fallen short. And it brings them great joy and happiness to see you lose your life.

Tea spillers, gossip sites, social media outlets, and more are like the "strongest" men who will bring you to the fire to watch you burn to be entertained. However, they fail to realize that the same fire they are carrying you to is the same flame that will kill them.

So, I say to you, stay faithful. No fire can burn you because He holds your hand.

Who or what has been a Nebuchadnezzar in your life?

Pray this prayer out loud: I refuse to be intimidated and pressured to worship anything or anyone that is not the Lord my God, Jesus Christ. Amen

Daytime confession:

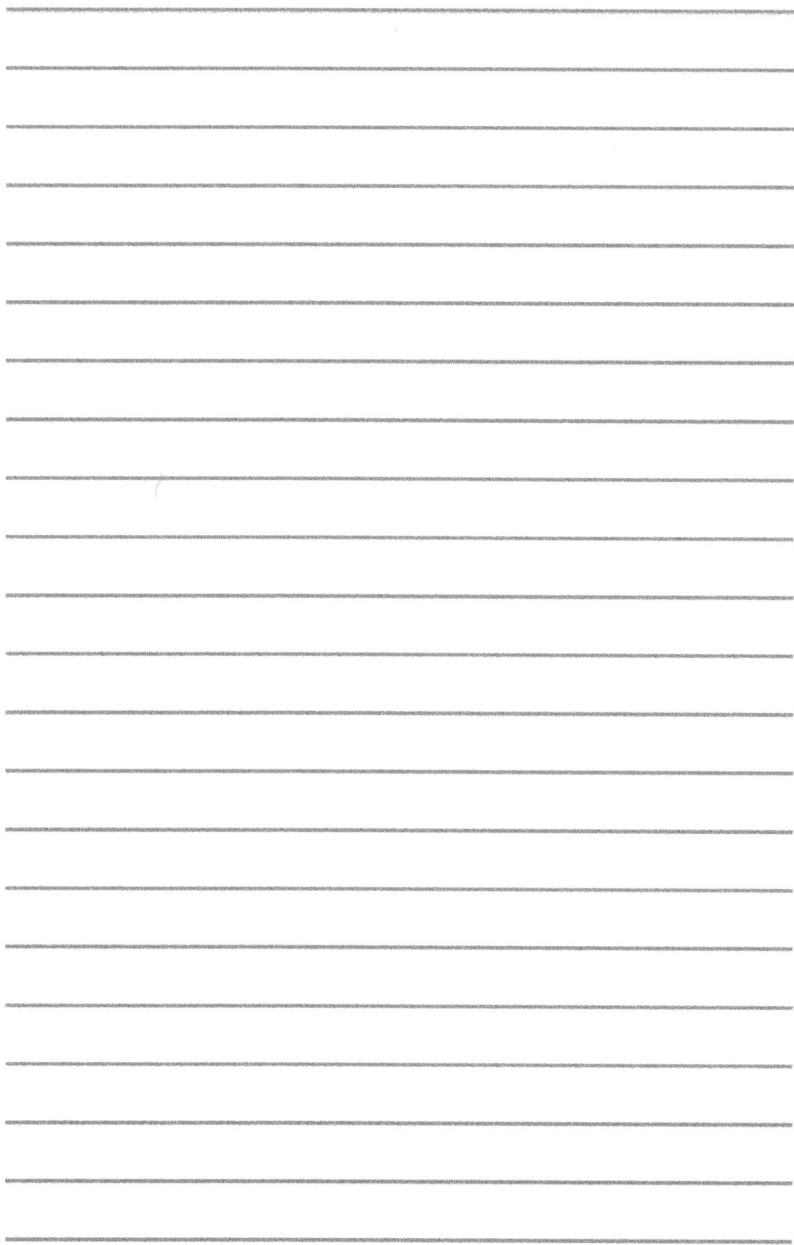

What types of things have you been made fun of and pressured into doing? Likewise, what things do you NOT do that get you teased and ridiculed?

Nighttime Confession:

DAY19

The Secret Place

I will show him My Salvation

He went in, therefore, shut the door behind the two of them, and prayed to the LORD. —2nd Kings 4:33 NKJV

When you are looking to have something in your life resurrected from the dead, you have to get into a space alone, with the door closed, activating faith, and crying out to the Lord until He gives you the instructions that will bring life back to that thing.

Today, we focus on activating a deeper level of faith in your life. Think of something inside you that has died, for example, your belief in Godly love and relationships, talents that you have used, dreams that you once had, etc.

Now that you have an idea of those dead things, read the passage from 2 Kings 4:8-37.

List the dead thing(s) in your life. How did they die?

Say this prayer out loud: Holy Spirit, I invite you into the dead parts of my heart, mind, body, soul, and spirit, and I receive the breath of life. In Jesus' Mighty name. Amen.

Daytime confession:

After reading the passage, how can you apply the action and prayer of Elisha to the dead thing(s) in your life?

Nighttime Confession:

DAY 20

I Will See The Goodness of the Lord

The Lord is the Stronghold of my Life

My brethren, count it all joy when you fall into various trials, knowing that the testing of your faith produces patience. James 1:2-3 NKJV

The Truth is a life in the daily pursuit of the Lord Jesus Christ that comes with daily rejection, persecution, slander, mockery, and various other trials and tribulations.

The Word tells us this upfront before anything recognizable as trials manifest themselves to us.

Here is where, *"the genuineness of your faith, being much more precious than gold that perishes, though it is tested by fire, may be found to praise, honor, and glory at the revelation of Jesus Christ, whom having not seen you love. 1 Peter 1:7 also Is tested showing the Lord how diligent you are "to present yourself approved to God, a worker who does not need to be ashamed, rightly dividing the word of truth." 2 Timothy 2:15 NKJV*

In this journey that you are on every day in which you engage, read, and meditate on The Word of God, you are preparing and positioning yourself for the trial that is to come. Once the trial begins, if you have been diligent in reading and meditating on The Word, practicing daily repentance, and giving Him all your cares, worries, and anxieties, you will find yourself with *"the peace of God, which surpasses all understanding, that will guard your hearts and minds through Christ Jesus."* Philippians 4:7 NKJV

What problem(s) have you seemed to have happen repetitively? How often does the problem seem to occur?

Pray this prayer out loud: Heavenly Father, I invite you into the trials in my life to examine and expose the error of my ways that have kept my expansion paralyzed. By faith, I reach out my hand to You and receive the answers to pass my trials and elevation to the next level. In Jesus' mighty name, I pray. Amen.

Daytime confession:

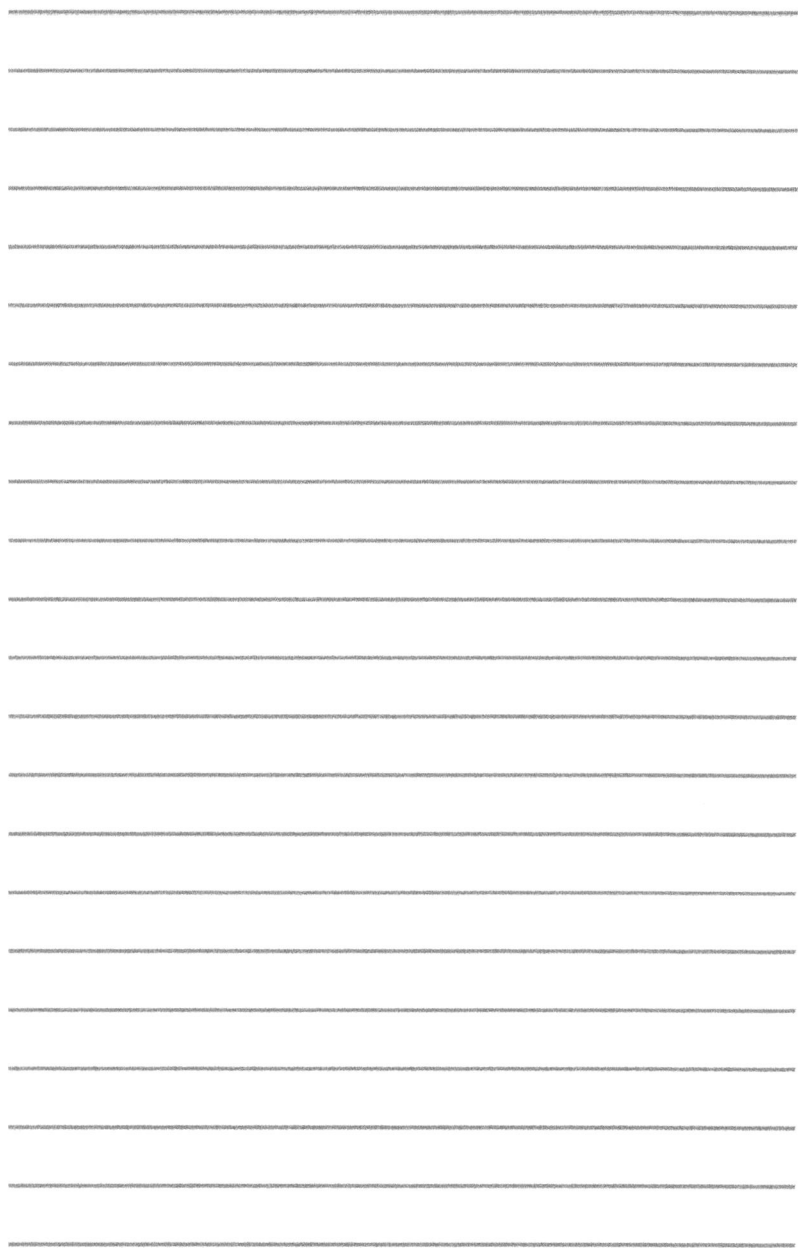

What have you done to survive or remedy the recurring problems in your life?

Nighttime confession:

DAY 21

I Will Repay

Avenge Not Yourself

"Is not My word like a fire?" says the LORD, "And like a hammer that breaks the rock in pieces? —Jeremiah 23:29 NKJV

The Word of God is a spiritual warfare weapon. And like any weapon in the physical world, you need to be trained in how to use it.

Basic training in the use of The Word of God starts in your mind, heart, body, and soul. Many Christians fail to realize the firepower of the written text of God when it is spoken out of their mouths.

The concept of this should be easily understood and supported by numerous texts, such as, *"Death and life are in the power of the tongue, and those who love it will eat its fruit."* - Proverbs 18:21. However, this verse is often softened in meaning, and the translation of it in the soul often gets lost in transmission when communicating instructions from God from the spirit to the body.

Think about it this way - when using a knife, represents the Word of God, *"For the word of God is living and powerful, and sharper than any two-edged sword, piercing even to the division of soul and spirit, and of joints and marrow, and is a discerner of the thoughts and intents of the heart."* - Hebrews 4:12

And with that knife, you cut an orange. The outer layer of the orange represents your body; the white area underneath represents the soul and the sweet part of the orange represents your spirit. The knife has to cut the outer layer, which is bitter and needs to be discarded. This layer is the layer you have to fight daily with the fire of God, for as it is written, *"The spirit indeed is willing, but the flesh is weak." Mark 14:38 NKJV*

Moving on, the white layer can be bitter, yet it can also have some sweet attached as it is in direct contact and the center layer in between the sweet and bitter layers. The soul is two-faced, as it has the ability to decide whether or not to obey the spirit - which would be the very thin layer of white that takes in the sweet taste. It can also be thick with the white layer, taking in more of the bitterness from the skin, which would be the soul obeying the body. Moreover, the representation of the orange is the battle that you will face every day. You choose whether to take the sweet part of God's Way using His sword and fire.

Depending on how you choose to dissect the orange will determine how much bitterness vs. sweetness you will receive. The battle in your mind, body, and soul is the first trial in which you "show yourself approved" and engage in this warfare to fight the good fight. *"Therefore, take up the whole armor of God, that you may be able to withstand in the evil day, and having done all, to stand."*- *Ephesians 6:13*

What thoughts, temptations, and emotional battles do you have daily?

Pray this prayer out loud: Holy Spirit I come to the throne to submit my heart mind, body, and spirit for examination, and I submit my will, intellect, emotions, and knowledge to You. Lead me in the way I should go. In Jesus' name. Amen.

Daytime confession:

_____

_____

_____

_____

_____

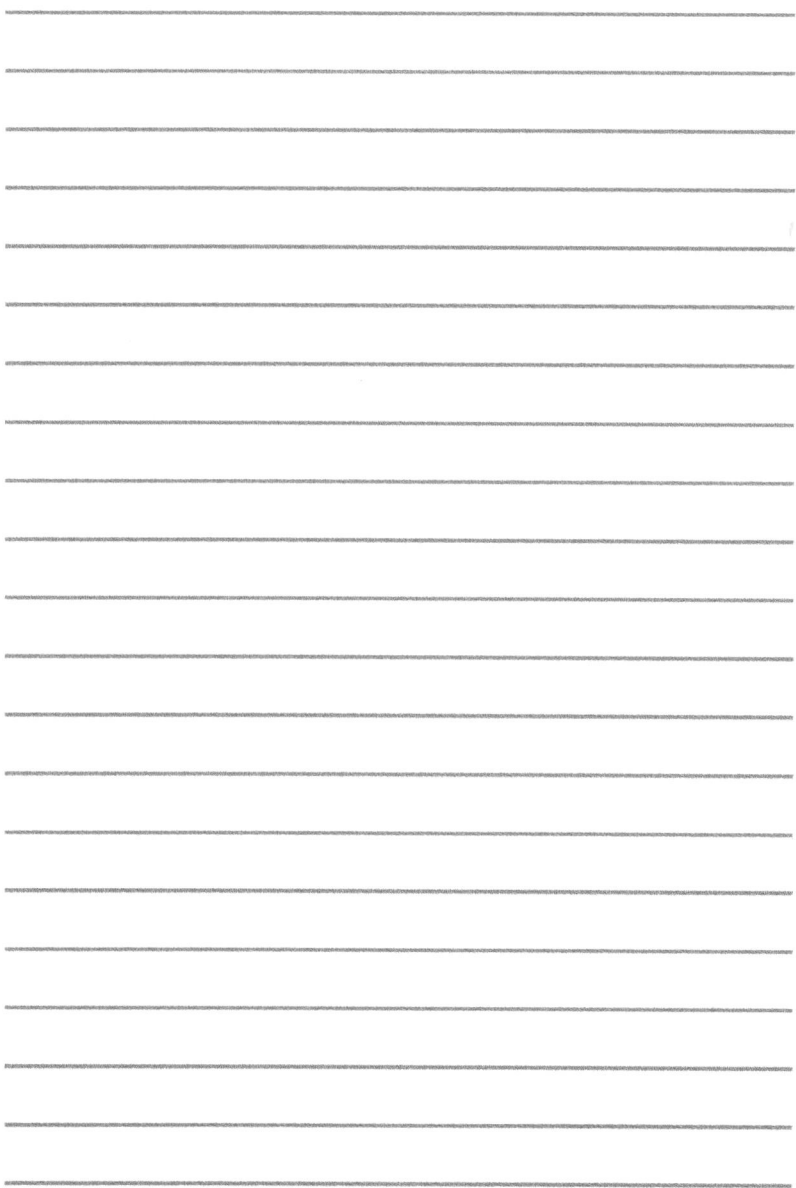

How often do you win vs. lose the mental, emotional, and temptation battles? Are you ready to do it God's way? If yes, why? If no, why not?

Nighttime Confession:

_____

_____

_____

_____

_____

_____

_____

_____

_____

_____

_____

_____

_____

_____

_____

_____

_____

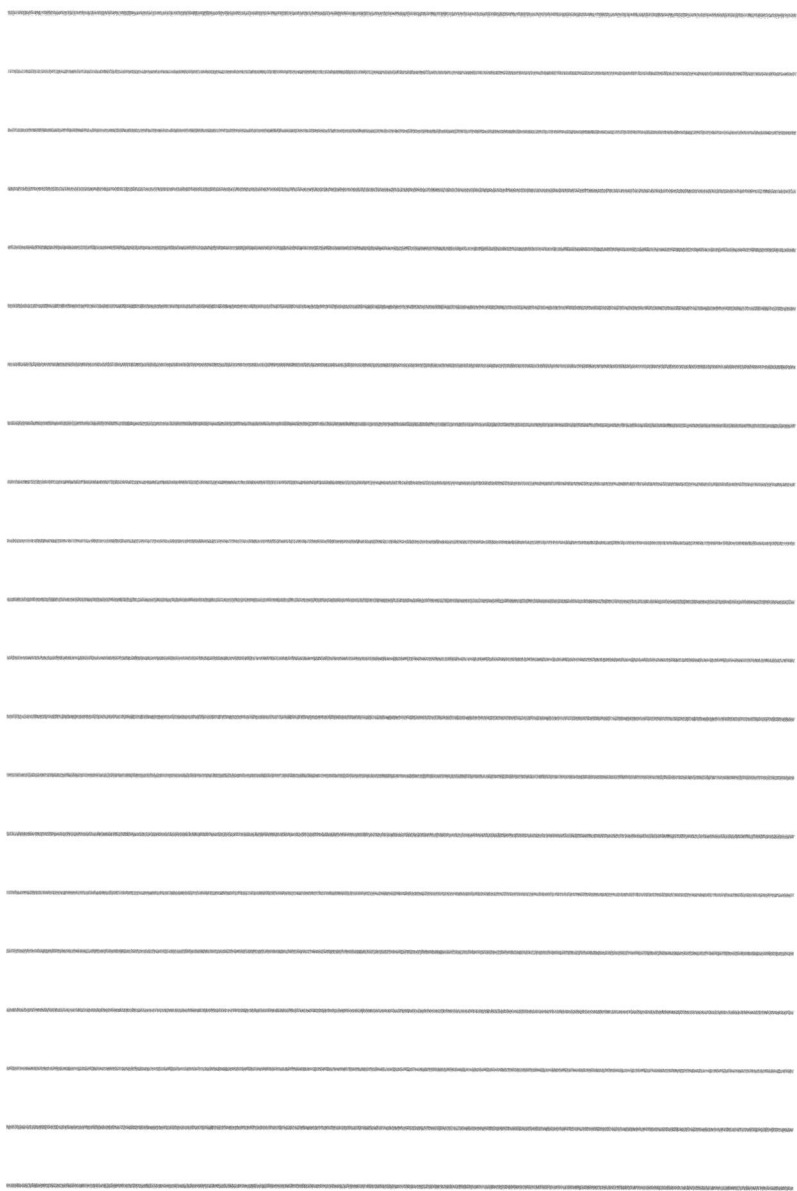

DAY 22

An Army Is Rising Up

No one engaged in warfare entangles himself with the affairs of this life

For we do not wrestle against flesh and blood, but against principalities, against powers, against the rulers of the darkness of this age, against spiritual hosts of wickedness in the heavenly places. Ephesians 6:12 NKJV

The whole armor of God is a must-have in your pursuit of the Lord daily. Why? Today's scripture gives you the answer. Additionally, there are things seen and unseen that we will battle, and much of this will come in the mind, thoughts, and heart.

Have you ever noticed that you can go so long and hard for the Lord? Praising, worshiping, and cutting people and things out of your life then - boom! You're flooded with thoughts of those things. Or all of a sudden, the hours in the day seem to fly by that you no longer have the same amount of time to praise, worship, or go to church?

This is not a coincidence. What you can't see are the entities in today's scripture, working even harder to find ways to manipulate areas of your life that you have yet given over to God - things you don't know to give to God and things you have already given to God, but the temptation to go back to what He has delivered you from increases.

One topic that may resonate with you is an old flame. Maybe this was someone who hurt you, and you had to make the decision to move on. Or maybe this is someone who you hurt, and they made the decision to move on. After years have passed, either way, you find yourself thinking about this person, looking them up on social media, running into them, or dreaming about them. All of this is a form of warfare that the enemy uses to gain legal grounds into your life to keep you going in circles and prevent you from moving on to the greater things that God has for you in His perfect will.

You combat this by daily putting on your armor of God that has been given to you to withstand the wiles of the devil. Literally, say the words: "*I activate the full armor of God, helmet of salvation, breastplate of righteousness, belt of truth, shield of faith, sandals of peace, sword of the Spirit, and the gift of speaking in the Spirit.*"

In doing so, you activate a level of shielding and protection from fire arrows that are sent out from the enemy's camp to bring you to level zero. The more you study this scripture, the more that the Holy Spirit will teach you how to use the armor to trample over the battles in your life.

What were you taught about how to handle the powers of darkness? Who taught you this?

Pray this prayer out loud: Holy Spirit, I surrender everything that I thought I knew about your word and things I was taught, and I invite you to re-teach me Your Word and extract out of me all that was taught incorrectly. In Jesus' Mighty name.

Daytime confession:

_____

_____

_____

_____

_____

_____

_____

What has the Holy Spirit taught you after meditating on today's scripture? How has that started to change how you see The Word of God?

Nighttime Confession:

_____

_____

_____

_____

_____

_____

_____

_____

_____

_____

_____

_____

_____

_____

_____

_____

DAY 23

Principles of War

You therefore must endure hardship as a good soldier

of Jesus Christ

When you go out to battle against your enemies, and see horses and chariots and people more numerous than you, do not be afraid of them; for the LORD your God is with you, who brought you up from the land of Egypt.

Deuteronomy 20:1 NKJV

One song that is on my warfare Playlist is called, *Surrounded (Fight my Battles)* by Michael W. Smith. The verse of this song that comes to mind when reading today's scripture is: "*It may look like I'm surrounded, but I'm surrounded by You.*"

The power in this lyric perfectly activates this scripture in the form of the weapon of praise. Yes, praise and worship are spiritual warfare weapons.

And the best time to use this weapon is at the beginning of the battle when it looks like you're surrounded by nothing other than brick walls, or you feel like you're about to drown in all the problems that are happening at once.

We co-labor in the fight by activating our faith and giving praise to the Lord. In this, He hears your heart's cries, and He goes into battle with you - even in the midst of the battle your praise will provoke the Lord to move on your behalf. If you surrender all of your own self-defense tactics, confess your weakness without Him, and believe that He is with you no matter what you see, around that says you're going to lose - you're going to win every time you allow the Lord to be your Shield and Mighty Buckler.

What battle are you facing right now? What praise and worship song comes to mind as you think of that battle?

Pray this prayer out loud: Holy Spirit, I surrender all to you - everything I give to you from my own arsenal of self-defense weapons. I lay them down at your feet, inviting You in to be my shield and mighty buckler. In Jesus' name. Amen.

Daytime confession:

What did you experience as you surrendered your self-defense weapons to Holy Spirit? What challenges occurred today that challenged how you defend yourself?

Nighttime Confession:

DAY 24

The Lord your God who goes before, you will fight for you

Helmet of Salvation

For the weapons of our warfare are not carnal but mighty in God for pulling down strongholds, casting down arguments and every high thing that exalts itself against the knowledge of God, bringing every thought into captivity to the obedience of Christ, and being ready to punish all disobedience when your obedience is fulfilled. 2 Corinthians 10:4-6 NKJV

The days to prepare for battle are here as the return of our Lord and Savior nears.

Many of us in training need to know what the weapons are and how to use them.

The daily verse is what we will meditate on today.

Weapons in the (CARNAL mind) are defined as a thing designed or used for inflicting bodily harm or physical damage OR a means of gaining an advantage or defending oneself in a conflict or contest.

Therefore, the carnal believer or unbeliever's mind can only comprehend the natural world in which we live (the definition is supported by practical experience of "physical" world things. What they see with their eyes.)

Maturing believers grasp the concept that there is a spiritual and natural world connecting the verse prior to this, as evidence which states, *"For though we walk in the flesh, we do not [war] according to the flesh." 2 Cor. 10:3*

Meaning that we live in the natural world in physical bodies that you can see with your skin, hair, nails, body, etc. - A*ll* of *which is flesh.*

However, when you are born again, you become a "new creature" and the old passes away. Furthermore, you die to yourself, killing the flesh and living through Christ in you.

Moreover, as you grow in The Word, which is "living and powerful," it continues to pierce (go into or through), separating your spirit, soul, and body (flesh).

Additionally, as we are separated from the flesh, our minds become more in tune with the mind of God, which allows our spirit to be led by the Holy Spirit.

Leading us to spiritual warfare, which is the battle of protecting our minds, thoughts, spirit, and soul from the deception of the enemy, this is why Jesus ALWAYS quoted scripture. Because it is a discerner of spirits, and it activates the "living and powerful two-edged sword," which is designed to inflict spiritual damage to the spirits (demons) that hold themselves as higher spirits - higher than the Most High God who is Spirit - the Holy Spirit.

So, when someone comes carnally with their opinions, arguments, and insults, the maturing believer recognizes this, and uses The Word of God as a shield and buckler, casting down arguments and exhalation above God. Demons hate this, and by this, you know the spirit behind the person.

What was the last argument you had? What were you offended by in that argument?

Pray this prayer out loud: Lord Jesus, I invite you into the area of my heart, mind, body, and soul to expose in me all areas of offense that I have acted on in the past or my present, and I ask you to pluck these roots out and replace it with Your Vine. Amen.

Daytime confession:

_____

_____

_____

_____

_____

_____

_____

_____

_____

_____

_____

_____

Have you forgiven the last person you got in an argument with? If not, why not? If yes, why?

Nighttime Confession:

_____

_____

_____

_____

_____

_____

_____

_____

_____

_____

_____

_____

_____

_____

_____

_____

_____

DAY 25

Do Not be Terrified or Afraid of them

Be Strong and of **G**ood **C**ourage

Today you are on the verge of battle with your enemies. Do not let your heart faint, do not be afraid, and do not tremble or be terrified because of them; for the LORD your God is He who goes with you, to fight for you against your enemies, to save you. Deuteronomy 20:3-4 NKJV

As human beings, our physical bodies get tired, requiring rest in order to function properly. However, our spirits are not bound by the same limitations.

The solution to continuing to fight even when your body is weak depends on your ability to praise and worship.

The ability to worship in Spirit and Truth is critical in the form of actions that you have to take when you have no physical strength in your body and soul. The enemy knows that you're limited by the physical body; therefore, the attack will begin by making sure your physical body is fatigued.

You know this to be true if you think about a time when you have been physically exhausted - maybe from a workout, a double shift, playing a sport, or non-stop errand running. In this state, what do you want to do most when you rest? You may want to kick up your feet, lay down, relax, and just not do anything or see anyone.

However, it is in this state that the enemy takes advantage because you're not usually thinking about anything related to praising the Lord. And that is when fear, anxiety, worry, and stress try to consume you and can affect how you sleep. And a lack of sleep for the physical body affects how fast you move as well as mental exhaustion. Therefore, practice praising during your weakest state -when everything on you hurts, you're not sleeping, and your problems seem to be piling up. Diligence in this area will have Jehova turning your life around.

Read Deuteronomy 20and write below what the Lord did in this passage. What introduction did He give? How did He lead the people to victory?

Pray this prayer out loud: Holy Spirit, I invite you into this study time and ask you to reveal the mystery of Your Word in which I can apply to my life right now. In Jesus' name. Amen.

Daytime Confession:

_____

_____

_____

_____

_____

_____

_____

_____

_____

_____

_____

_____

_____

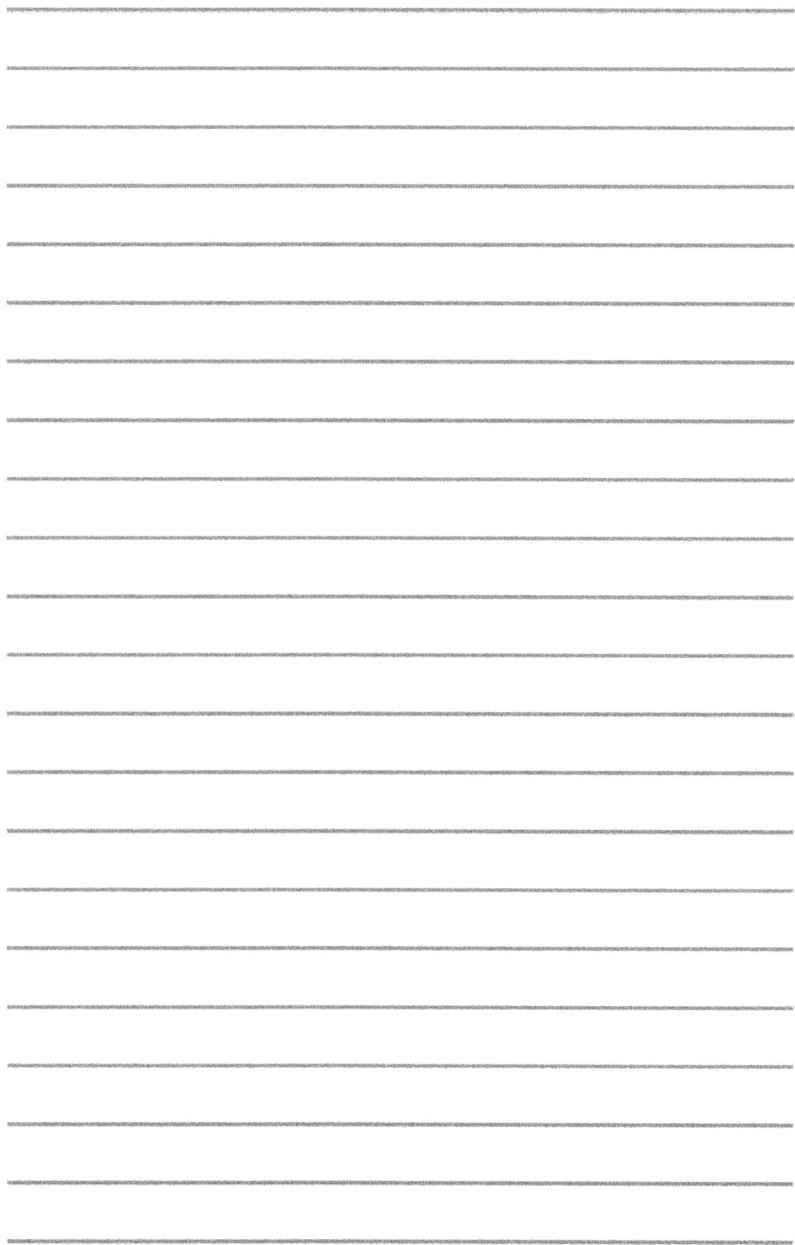

What are the governing principles of warfare that the Lord states in this chapter?

Nighttime confession:

DAY 26

You shall Tread upon the lion and the cobra

The young lion and the serpents you shall trample underfoot

> *Behold, I give you the authority to trample on serpents and scorpions, and over all the power of the enemy, and nothing shall by any means hurt you. Luke 10:19 NKJV*

Jesus said it best, *"I say to you, he who believes in Me, the works that I do he will do also; and greater works than these he will do because I go to My Father. - John 14:12*

The authority that He gave to you, He displayed in several ways during His 3-year ministry in the flesh on Earth. In Mark 1:21-28 NKJV, Jesus cast out a demon in a man sitting in the place of worship.

Once He commanded the unclean spirit to leave the man, he was made well. *"Then they were all amazed, so that they questioned among themselves, saying, "What is this? What new doctrine is this? For with authority He commands even the unclean spirits, and they obey Him." Mark 1:27 NKJV*

After several occurrences of this, even His 70 followers were overjoyed that demons were subject to them in the name of Jesus, and He replied, *"Nevertheless, do not rejoice in this, that the spirits are subject to you, but rather rejoice because your names are written in heaven."-Luke 10:20 NKJV*.

Of course, this is just one of many deliverance, healing, signs, and wonders that He performed in His flesh life, and as He did, so did His faithful followers.

How faithful you are in following Him determines the level of authority in His name you unlock in your life. Gaining authority is like going to school. If you do not study and participate in the grade-level lessons, you'll be left behind.

What questions do you have about accessing authority in Jesus' name?

Say this prayer out loud: Holy Spirit, I invite you into this study time, and I ask that you reveal to me the answers to my questions, teaching me how to grow in authority to complete my assignment in Your perfect will. In Jesus' name. Amen.

Daytime Confession:

_____

_____

_____

_____

_____

_____

_____

_____

_____

_____

_____

_____

_____

_____

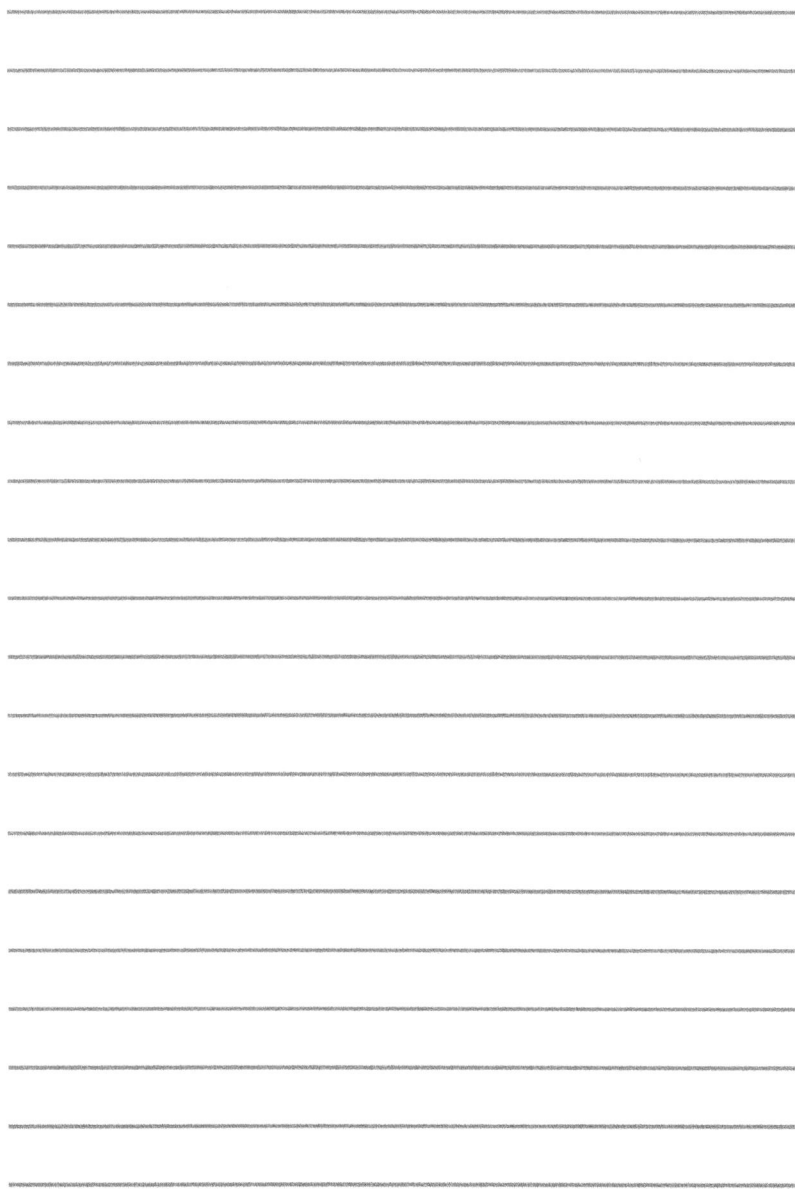

What are heirs entitled to? In what ways have you lived as an heir of salvation? Or not?

Nighttime confession:

_____

_____

_____

_____

_____

_____

_____

_____

_____

_____

_____

_____

_____

_____

_____

_____

_____

_____

_____

DAY 27

Behold, I have Inscribed You on the palms of My hands

Your walls are continuously before me

My Father, who has given them to Me, is greater than all; and no one is able to snatch them out of My Father's hand. I and My Father are one."
John 10:29-30

As an heir of salvation, *"In Him you also trusted, after you heard the word of truth, the gospel of your salvation; in whom also, having believed, you were sealed with the Holy Spirit of promise, who is the guarantee of our inheritance until the redemption of the purchased possession, to the praise of His glory."*
Ephesians 1:13

This means that you have been marked and sealed by the blood that Jesus shed on the cross and have received the gift of eternal life when He rose on the third day.

The reality is that NOT everyone in the world is sealed with the promises of the Holy Spirit, though they do have the ability to receive it with belief and confession that Jesus Christ is Lord.

Today's word is an encouraging reminder from the mouth of Jesus, Himself, that no matter what challenges you face, in the daily pursuit of Him, you are engraved in the palm of His hand - and NO ONE can take you from Him. Be encouraged, for the kingdom of God is at hand.

When was the last time you felt that God abandoned you or forgot about you?

Pray this prayer out loud: Lord Jesus, I come to the Thrown of Mercy to confess and release my anger, bitterness, and unbelief towards you. I invite you into this space to open up my heart and heal me of this pain I feel you have caused me. In Jesus' name. Amen.

Daytime confession:

_____

_____

_____

_____

_____

List and discuss all the reasons why God would not forgive you or hear your anger towards Him.

Nighttime Confession:

_____

_____

_____

_____

_____

_____

_____

_____

_____

_____

_____

_____

_____

_____

_____

_____

_____

_____

_____

_____

_____

_____

_____

DAY 28

A Son Abides Forever

He who is called in the Lord while a slave is the Lords

freedman

Therefore, you are no longer a slave but a son, and if a son, then an heir of God through Christ.

Galatians 4:7 NKJV

Slaves - in any context that you can think of in history - have a common theme of chains and shackles.

Do you remember the word from the book of Mark, chapter 5, and the story about the demon-possessed man and how he had often been bound with "chains and shackles?" These chains and shackles had been placed on him in the physical world, and they could not contain him because our text states, *"And the chains had been pulled apart by him, and the shackles broken in pieces; neither could anyone tame him." Mark 5:4*

However, in the realm of the unseen, this man was in chains and shackles of the powers of darkness, in which we learn the name of these powers as a "legion." Legion, meaning thousands of demons, places them as a higher-ranking demon entity.

Due to this, Jesus had to display the ultimate authority he has over "high ranking" demons, giving us a practical application of the levels of inheritance we can attain as sons and heirs of God through Christ.

Remembering this scripture and meditating on it will begin to shatter the shackles that are binding you in the unseen realm. Receive your freedom as it is written, *"whosoever the Son has set free is free indeed." John 8:36 NKJV*

Have you felt a heaviness over your body, in your mind, or your heart that you can't explain? Describe the feelings and effects that it had on you.

Pray this prayer out loud: I break and loose myself from every demonic chain and shackle that is holding me down by the authority and the blood and name of Jesus Christ. And I refuse to be chained down again in the name of Jesus. Amen.

Daytime confession:

Pray this prayer out loud:

I renounce all agreements that I have made in the past or in my present that have me bound in chains and shackles in the demonic kingdom. Lord, I thank You for Your love for me, and I put my trust in You. I dip this room and myself in the blood of Jesus. Holy Spirit, take over this deliverance. You demons in my body, I revoke your residency in me, in the name of Jesus.

Write what happened to you as you said this prayer. What revelation did you come to after this experience? (tingling, crying, dry mouth, headache, spitting, shaking, vomiting, etc.)

Nighttime confession:

_____

_____

_____

_____

_____

_____

_____

_____

_____

_____

_____

_____

Free Expression

DAY 29

He who is joined to the Lord is One Spirit with Him

Glorify God in body and spirit

But now we have been delivered from the law, having died to what we were held by, so that we should serve in the newness of the Spirit and not in the oldness of the letter. Romans 7:6 NKJV

Daily crucifixion of the flesh leads to the death of the old person, ways, and passions you used to engage in.

As a new creature with the old being dead, you have been delivered from standard laws of old that fed the passions and lust of our former bodies because we did not understand how to abide by those laws, making them corrupt.

When Jesus came in the flesh, died, and rose again on the third day, His physical presence and the length of time He walked the earth in the flesh was the exact length of time needed to re-teach by example. With His actions, He displayed how to properly obey the law, which was fixed, and in the resurrection, making the law active and alive with the newness of the Spirit of God - freeing us from the bondage created by man from the oldness of the law from the old testament. The merging of the Old Testament and New Testament's practical application carried out by Jesus in each story, creates the newness of the Spirit and a revelation of the mystery of the law as God intended for them to be kept from the beginning.

Read this Romans 7:
What have you learned from this passage?

Heavenly Father, send Your Holy Spirit to open my eyes to understand Your Word in this study time, in the name of Jesus.

Daytime confession:

Read the Romans 7:

What is something new that sticks out to you that you didn't catch before?

Nighttime Confession:

DAY 30

Renew Your spiritual Vitality

Chadesh (Hebrew). Renew.

And do not be conformed to this world, but be transformed by the renewing of your mind, that you may prove what is that good and acceptable and perfect will of God. Romans 12:2 NKJV

Renewing [YOUR] Salvation

Carnal Christians amaze me daily with their elementary principles and concepts about the Spirit of God and His doctrine.

Furthermore, it deeply troubles my spirit to witnesses, in 2021, the countless Christians who have been given seed (watered down, manipulated) Word of God from "Sowers" (Bishops, preachers, teachers, minsters, etc.), who have sown seed by the wayside, stony places, and thorns. BUT God is TRUE to His Word, and FEW have been given seed on "good ground."

Moreover, in the last days, which are at hand, an army of relentless warriors of God have been risen to "teach you again the first principles of the oracles of God" because you have come to need milk and not solid food. For everyone who partakes only of milk is unskilled in the word of righteousness, for he is a babe. But solid food belongs to those who are of full age, that is, those who by reason of use have their senses exercised to discern both good and evil." Hebrews 5:12-13 NKJV

"Therefore, leaving the discussion of the elementary principles of Christ." Hebrews 6:1-3 NKJV

The Word says, "But of that [exact] day and hour no one knows, not even the angels of heaven, nor the Son [in His humanity], but the Father alone." Matthew 24:36 NKJV

Basic, common sense says, "IF NO ONE" knows the day or hour JESUS will return, *"And from there we eagerly await [the coming of] the Savior, the Lord Jesus Christ."* Phil. 3:20 THEN, I [YOU] must do something CONTINUALLY to maintain [YOUR] life with God. (Salvation) because He could appear at ANY second.

And in that second, if [YOU] have not repented and are in constant vigilance with a sober mind of RENEWING your Salvation, mind, and, crucifying your flesh; [YOU] will burn in HELL because He will say, "DEPART FROM ME, I NEVER KNEW YOU!" Matthew 7:23

Lastly, in the natural, you RENEW your license, registration, Netflix, Hulu, porn subscription, lease, health insurance, voter registration, passport, etc. And you walk around "believing your

Salvation doesn't need to be RENEWED." You're currently in line to hear those dreadful words from our Lord:

Repent daily, crucify your flesh daily, and turn from your wicked ways. Let those who have an ear LET them hear!

How has renewing your mind in this devotional benefited you so far?

Daytime Confession:

_____

_____

_____

_____

_____

_____

_____

_____

_____

_____

_____

_____

_____

How have your problems progressed as you've been renewing your mind in these past 30 days?

Nighttime confession:

_____

_____

_____

_____

_____

_____

_____

_____

_____

_____

_____

_____

_____

_____

_____

_____

_____

DAY 31

Law cannot Save from sin

.

I Delight in the law of God according to the inward man

> *For I know that in me (that is, in my flesh) nothing good dwells; for to will is present with me, but how to perform what is good I do not find. For the good that I will to do, I do not do; but the evil I will not to do, that I practice. Now if I do what I will not to do, it is no longer I who do it, but sin that dwells in me. Romans 7:18-20 NKJV*

As your thinking begins to shift throughout your daily meditation on The Word, you will start to find this scripture to be true.

Remember: you're in a battle of mind, body, and soul, and the first level of warfare begins with the self. Confession and conscious awareness of the sinful nature of soul and body becomes evident when you are doing what you think is right – especially when someone has said something that does not agree with you, and they want to continue pressing the issue until you find yourself in a full-fledged argument with them.

The 'tug' in that scenario that has pulled you into the argument is evidence that nothing good dwells in the flesh. We know this because, in your own will, you tried to avoid argument; however, the pressure to argue continued into the carnal self of the flesh, despite your effort to do it God's way.

How you conquer this sinful nature of flesh in you is by continuously confessing your weakness and offense to the Lord in your heart and mind.

In the example mentioned above, *in the midst of the back and forth going on*, you might think and or verbalize something like this, "Heavenly Father, this person is trying to get me to snap on them and I'm at the point of giving into it. I admit that I do not know how to respond in the way that you want me to. I surrender my mouth and words to you and ask you to send Your Holy Spirit to teach me how to get out of this Your way. In Jesus' name. Amen.

What are some good things you do or have done for others? Was it something God told you to do or something you did on your own?

Daytime confession:

_____

_____

_____

_____

_____

_____

_____

_____

_____

_____

_____

_____

_____

_____

_____

_____

_____

How do you know God is telling you to do something?

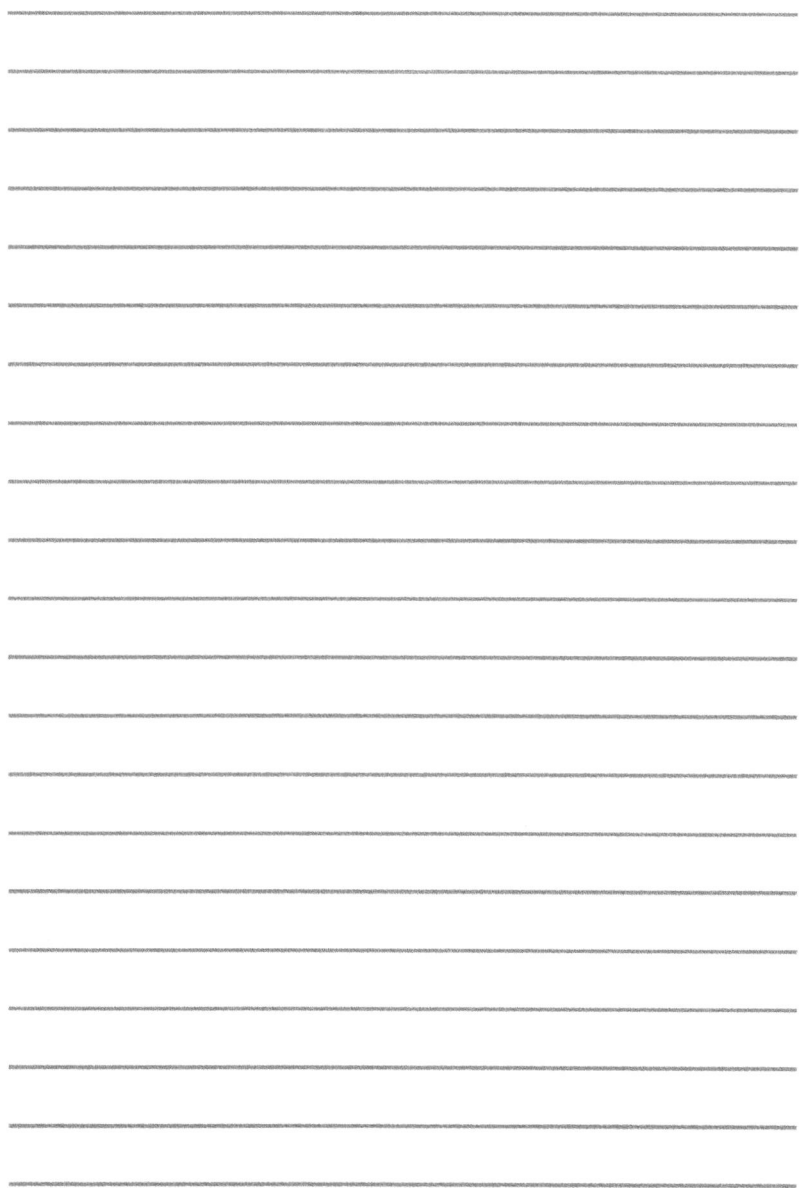

DAY 32

Unashamed

Follow Him

I affirm, by the boasting in you which I have in Christ Jesus our Lord, I die daily 1 Corinthians 15:31 NKJV

In Matthew: 16:24, Jesus says, *"If anyone desires to come after Me, let him deny himself, and take up his cross, and follow Me."*

One of the ways the cross is significant to us is by bearing our cross in pursuit of our Lord and Savior. This is found in Galatians 3:13: *"Christ has redeemed us from the curse of the law, having become a curse for us (for it is written, "Cursed is everyone who hangs on a tree"), that the blessing of Abraham might come upon the Gentiles in Christ Jesus, that we might receive the promise of the Spirit through faith." NKJV*

Therefore, by taking up our cross (which is also symbolic of death), we keep ourselves under the curse of the blood of Jesus, who died on the cross to redeem us and who rose on the 3rd day so that we may live eternally.

Daily death is required because we are a spirit that has a soul who lives in a sinful body, which must die in order to be reconciled to God.

In what ways can you die to self today?

Pray the prayer out loud: Holy Spirit, I submit my will, intellect, and knowledge to You. And as you to teach me what it means to die daily, I will follow You. In Jesus' name. Amen.

Daytime confession:

_____

_____

_____

_____

_____

_____

_____

_____

_____

_____

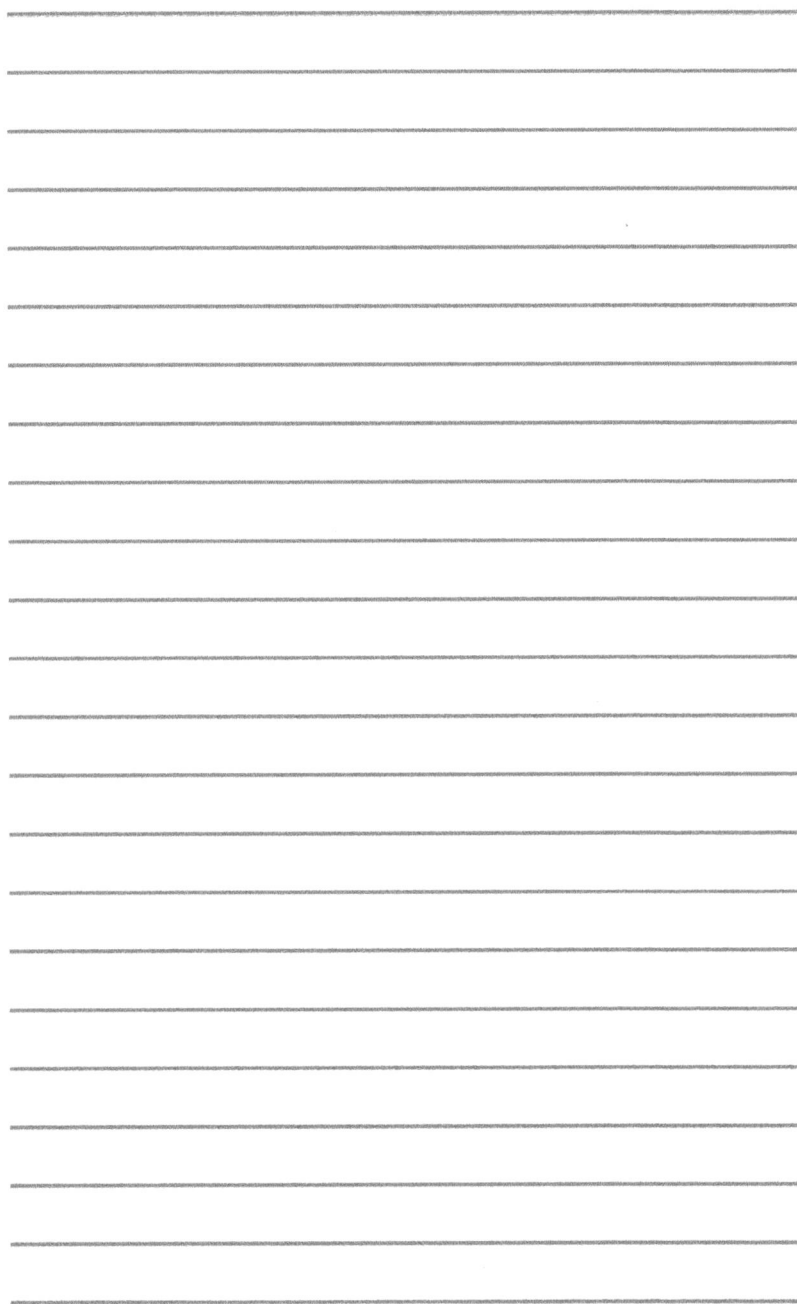

How was your experience of 'dying to self' today? What challenges did you face?

Nighttime Confession:

_____

_____

_____

_____

_____

_____

_____

_____

_____

_____

_____

_____

_____

_____

_____

_____

_____

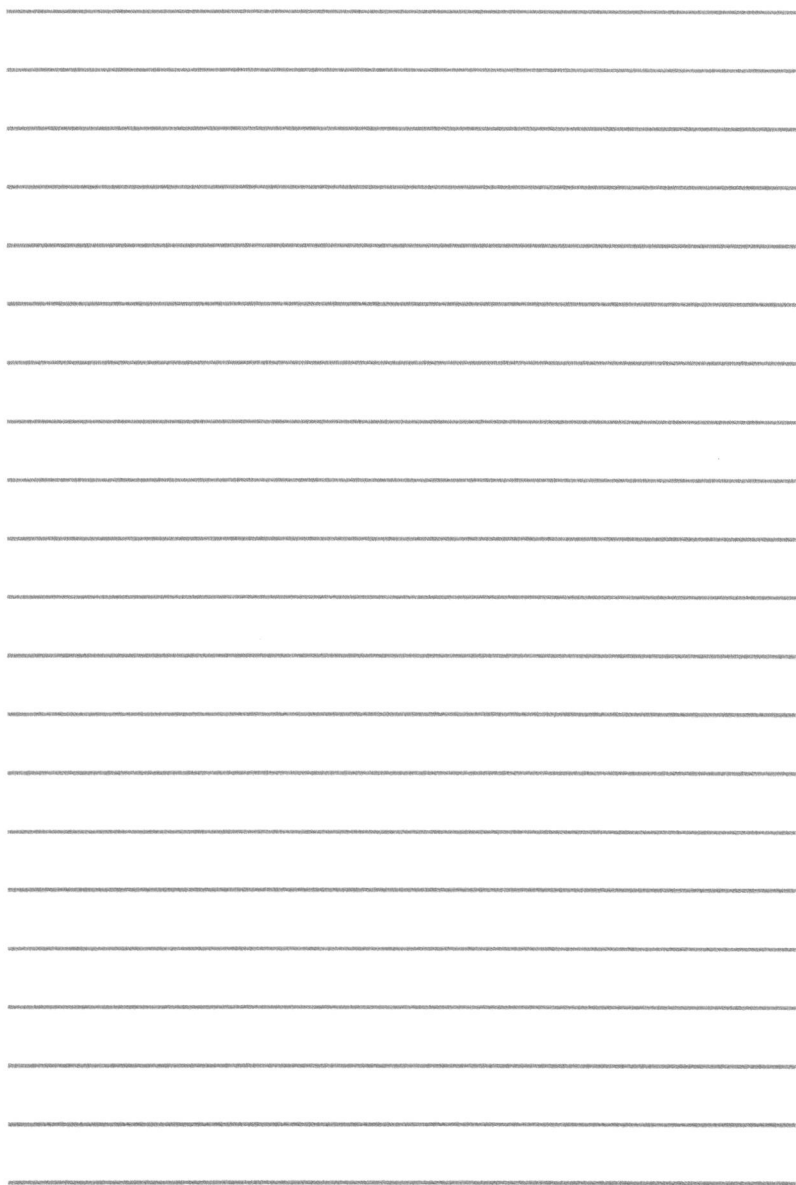

DAY 33

Some do not have the knowledge of God

Purge out the old leaven

Do not be deceived: "Evil company corrupts good habits." 1 Corinthians 15:33 NKJV

The challenges you will face as you practice renewing your mind and dying to self daily, will often come with a cutting off of friends and family who still engage in bad habits.

Are closest friends and family, who engage in premarital sex, lying, stealing, fighting, gossiping, argumentative, or practicing idolization in any way, starting to slowly fall away from your life?

The hard truth is that the habits of these people will significantly hinder your full maturation of growth and change. In this truth lies a battle as you begin to rationalize and think with your emotions in parallel to being told by God to cut people out of your life. The deception projected by the enemy will play on the state of rationalizing and making emotional decisions, not to follow the instructions of the Lord.

What things have you been seeking for God's help in changing your actions and behaviors?

Pray the prayer out loud: Holy Spirit, I submit my will, mind, intellect, knowledge, and emotions to you and ask you to reveal to me who I need to cut out of my life. In Jesus' name. Amen.

Daytime Confession:

_____

_____

_____

_____

_____

_____

_____

_____

_____

_____

Who has the Lord brought to your mind today to cut out of your life? What emotions do you have about this?

Nighttime Confession:

—

_____

_____

_____

_____

_____

_____

_____

_____

_____

_____

_____

_____

_____

_____

_____

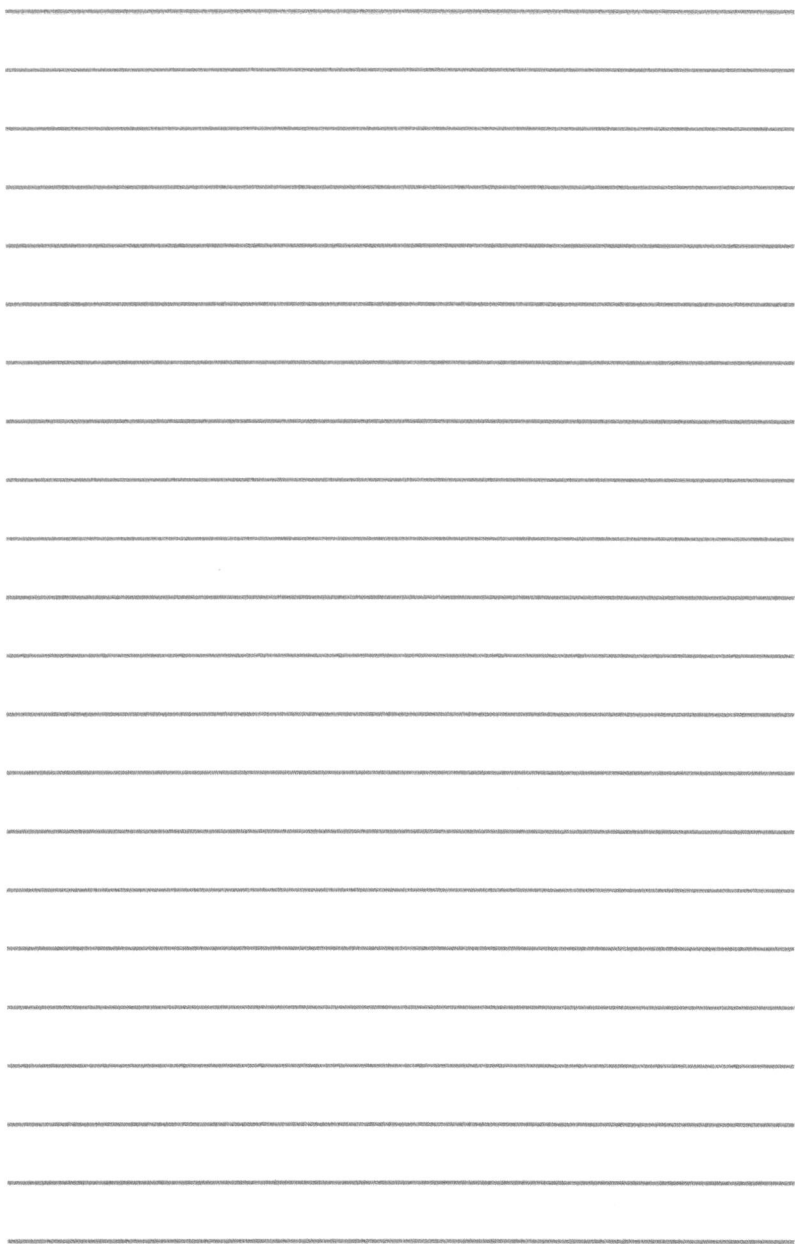

DAY 34

The Cost of Discipleship

What profit a man to gain the whole world and lose his soul?

Then He said to them all, "If anyone desires to come after Me, let him deny himself, and take up his cross daily, and follow Me. Luke 9:23 NKJV

Another lesson from this Holy Scripture is found in the context of the verses immediately following in Luke 9:24-26, "*For whoever desires to save his life will lose it, but whoever loses his life for My sake will save it. For what profit is it to a man if he gains the whole world, and is himself destroyed or lost? For whoever is ashamed of Me and My words, of him the Son of Man will be ashamed when He comes in His own glory, and in His Father's, and of the holy angels.*"

You have to be willing to LOSE *your life daily* and come under constant rejection, persecution, slander, mocking, reviling, and hated by family, friends, and the world. In doing so, for of Jesus

Christ and the *good news of the gospel*, your life will be saved eternally in the great and terrible day of the Lord.

However, a life that is not willing to die for His name's sake or the good news of the gospel will lose his life eternally in the great and terrible day of the Lord.

The message that is given in this text is your choice to die for His name and the Truth of His Word, earning access to heaven. Or losing your soul for the ways of the world and denying His word and earning eternal weeping and gnashing in Hell.

In what ways have you suffered persecution and rejection for His name? How did it make you feel?

Pray this prayer out loud: Lord Jesus, I invite you into the area of my heart that is faint and confess that I am weak without you. In my weakness, I declare that You become strong to endure until the end. In Jesus' name.

Daytime Confession:

What scares you about The Word and the name of Jesus at all times? What do you feel you're losing by doing so?

Nighttime Confession:

_____

_____

_____

_____

_____

_____

_____

_____

_____

_____

_____

_____

_____

_____

_____

DAY 35

A Little While longer

I go to prepare a place for you

The time is fulfilled, and the kingdom of God is at hand. Repent, and believe in the gospel." Mark 1:15 NKJV

The time to the end is quickly approaching, COVID, simultaneous global natural disasters, an increase in mass killings globally, and much more.

The urgency to repent and turn from wicked ways has never been pushed so hard, and it will only continue to be pushed to allow for more souls to be won to Christ.

I say to you that likewise there will be more joy in heaven over one sinner who repents than over ninety-nine just persons who need no repentance. Luke 15:7 NKJV

Messages of the Call and The Last Call on the lives of many people globally have already gone out. The Kingdom of God is at hand,

and those who do not answer the call to repentance will be left behind.

What challenges do you face with daily repentance?

Daytime confession:

_____

_____

_____

_____

_____

_____

_____

_____

_____

_____

_____

_____

_____

_____

_____

_____

How do you view daily repentance?

Nighttime Confession:

DAY 36

Sonship

You shall know the truth, and the truth shall set you
free

*Therefore, if the Son makes you free, you shall be free indeed. John 8:36
NKJV*

When you transition from a slave of sin to a son as an heir of
salvation through Christ Jesus, you become free by Jesus, who paid
the price for your freedom from sin.

Dwelling and abiding in His Word continuously renew the truth of
His Word in you, and by doing so, you maintain your freedom.

The more consistent you are with SEEKING THE TRUTH, the
greater levels of freedom you will unlock in your life.

In what ways are you still a slave to sin?

Daytime confession:

In what ways have you been set free from sin?

Nighttime Confession:

_____

_____

_____

_____

_____

_____

_____

_____

_____

_____

_____

_____

_____

_____

_____

_____

_____

DAY 37

Have Faith In God

Do Not Doubt In Your Heart

Therefore, I say to you, whatever things you ask when you pray, believe that you receive them, and you will have them. Mark 11:24 NKJV

Romans 8:24 states, *"For we were saved in this hope, but hope that is seen is not hope; for why does one still hope for what he sees?" NKJV*

Paul is speaking about our suffering for His Glory.

In this, it drives in the revelation that your salvation was granted by hope, belief, and faith - all of which are tangibly unseen. To hope for something that you can physically see is not hope when it comes to a life dedicated to the Lord your God.

Therefore, we must hope for what we do not see for as it is written, *"Blessed are those who have not seen and yet have believed." John 20:29 NKJV*

Your belief in Jesus Christ of Nazareth is the first act of hope unseen as you eagerly await the second coming, *"For our citizenship is in heaven, from which we also eagerly wait for the Savior, the Lord Jesus Christ, who will transform our lowly body that it may be conformed to His glorious body, according to the working by which He is able even to subdue all things to Himself."* Philippians 3:20-21 NKJV

Furthermore, you must continually challenge what makes you forget all the benefits of the gift of salvation through hope in Christ Jesus by washing your thoughts with the Truth of His Word.

Once you begin practicing this, you will be elevated to the next level. You will have been tested and approved by Him and begin unlocking the mystery and power of today's verse.

So, when you pray, pray in the spirit, for you do not know all the things to pray for. Next, hope as you hope in the return of the Lord to bring you into heaven for eternal life. And apply these things to everything that you want and need - even when there doesn't seem to be an open door to receive it. The door is open; you need to walk through it.

> *"He who has an ear, let him hear what the Spirit says."* Revelation 2:11
> NKJV

"I know your works. See, I have set before you an open door, and no one can shut it; for you have a little strength, have kept My word, and have not denied My name." Revelation 3:8

What are things that you cannot see in your life (stable income, deliverance, housing, mental, emotional support, etc.) in which you do not have, nor can you see, how you will obtain it?

Pray this prayer out loud: Holy Spirit, I submit my heart and brain to you and request that you tear down all memory cells and beliefs in the things unseen and replace it with Your Truth and Vine so I may stand in submission to you in this battle. In Jesus' Mighty name. Amen.

Daytime Confession:

_____

_____

_____

_____

_____

_____

_____

_____

_____

_____

Have you given up on the breakthrough of the things you revealed earlier in the day? Do you feel hopeless and helpless? If yes, why? If no, why not?

Nighttime Confession:

DAY 38

Born Again

The righteousness of faith speaks in this way

If you confess with your mouth the Lord Jesus and believe in your heart that God has raised Him from the dead, you will be saved. Romans 10:9 NKJV

One piece of proof that you need the gospel of His Word lies in Romans, chapter 10.

Skipping to verse 8 of this chapter, as it is written, "*But what does it say? "The word is near you, in your mouth and in your heart."* (That is, the word of faith, which we preach.)

This means that the Word of God must be engraved in your heart. Once it's there, it will be confessed with your mouth publicly and privately because, as a true believer in Christ Jesus, you activate the Living Word found in Romans 1:16: *"For I am not ashamed of the gospel of Christ, for it is the power of God to salvation for everyone who believes, for the Jew first and also for the Greek."* NKJV

The words that you speak have power, and the more you come into agreement with the written word and allow it to be engraved in your heart, the more your faith and hope will be unshakable and unmovable in Jesus' Mighty name. Amen.

When was the last time you believed that Jesus rose from the dead and is living? When was the last time you confessed this privately and publicly?

Daytime Confession:

When was the last time Jesus showed you He was living? What did he do? If you don't know if He has shown you He is living, why do you believe that?

Nighttime Confession:

DAY 39

The Last Call

Not by might nor by power but by the Spirit of God

And He said to me, "My grace is sufficient for you, for My strength is made perfect in weakness." 2 Corinthians 12:9 NKJV

Sometimes, the Lord will allow a level of discomfort to remain in your life as a thorn.

He allows this so we are not tempted to fall victim to self-exaltation, forgetting that we are weak and can do nothing without Him.

If we have no constant reminder of affliction in our members, then the death and resurrection of our Lord Jesus would become weakened in your life and brings you back to a place of idolization or self-idolization.

Therefore, continued confession with your mouth of your weakness without Him becomes critical in granting you the full manifestation of His Grace and strength.

Read 2nd Corinthians, chapter 12. What thoughts about yourself came to mind when you came across the section dealing with the thorn in the flesh?

Daytime confession:

_____

_____

_____

_____

_____

_____

_____

_____

_____

_____

_____

_____

_____

What thorn was revealed to you earlier in the day? How does the Lord want you to use that for your divine assignment? If you do not have the answer, ask the Lord to reveal it to you, then answer the first two questions.

Nighttime Confession:

_____

_____

_____

_____

_____

_____

_____

_____

_____

_____

_____

_____

_____

_____

_____

DAY 40

God Is Testing You

🕊️

For in YAH, the LORD, Is Everlasting Strength

You will keep him in perfect peace, whose mind is stayed on You, because he trusts in You. Isaiah 26:3 NKJV

Focus is what today's scripture comes down to. Think of it as the active time you spend on IG, FB, and other social media outlets.

On those platforms, they give you a tab titled: "your activity. " And under that tab, is stored *how much time you spend engag*ing on that platform *and look*ing at, *liked, shared, commented on* content. *This information then goes on to be stored in algorithms that create personal* explorer pages, *which are suggestions based of the things you engage* during "your activity" time.

The Word of God is the most powerful platform you could use to engage with - and the only platform that has the ability to preserve your soul from the depths of Hell.

Jesus Christ is the head algorithm, and the content He displays for you to engage creates a custom explorer page that is active and alive, piercing and separating your soul from your spirit so you may live eternally.

God the Father is the overseer of your Heavenly activity time, seeing everything you do in pursuit of Him or not.

The moral of this scripture is: *the higher your heavenly activity time the more peace mentally, emotionally, and spiritually you will have.*

Look at your social media activity time. How much of a difference is there between social media time and Bible studying time daily?

Daytime confession:

_____

_____

_____

_____

_____

_____

_____

_____

After completing the 40 days and 40 nights, how much peace have you emotionally, mentally and spiritually? Have you been able to handle trails better as you've worked your way through this devotional?

Nighttime confession:

_____

_____

_____

_____

_____

_____

_____

_____

_____

_____

_____

_____

_____

_____

_____

_____

Notes and Reflections

About the Author

Da'Naia Jackson has been filled with a fresh anointing while under the inspiration of the Holy Spirit. Healing God's Way is this author's first fruit offered to the Lord for bringing her through a multitude of trials and tribulations.

She is a 4th generation evangelist from three sides of her family and first-time author of the teaching of the gospel of Christ Jesus.

Visit Evangelist Da'Naia's Ministry to find out more about her books at www.danaiajacksonministries.com